"Radical. Compelling. Timeless. Timely. Po   ıy's
vision for what it means to be a woman is

                        N   :hor
                                                  host

"Kristen and Bethany are great role models. And this message   Who
doesn't wonder if they are 'enough'? This book will redefine what it means to be a girl."

"In a day when women are confused about their value and identity, they desperately need to know that the only one who can define them is the One who created them! In *Girl Defined*, Kristen Clark and Bethany Baird point women to the true definition of their worth and to the ultimate freedom that comes from femininity defined by God. *Girl Defined* is on point! This book is a timely and needed read for women of all ages!"

"This book is for every girl who has ever looked in the mirror and asked, 'Am I pretty?' For every sports-lovin', pink-shunning girl who has ever wondered how she could fit into God's mold for womanhood. For every girl with a secret yearning to turn heads everywhere she goes. God's girls everywhere, this book is for you!"

"Beauty, sexuality, gender identity, purpose, and value are being defined by the shallow standards of our culture. But two young writers are bravely challenging the status quo and calling women to embrace true beauty and womanhood—as defined by God. Kristen and Bethany are painfully transparent as they invite us into their life experiences and show us how to live out the glorious purpose God has for us as women! *Girl Defined* is a carefully researched book that leads women to think through their purpose on a grand and biblical scale."

"Women today are told that their value is sexual. They have worth because of their beauty, and they should use their looks to gain power over men. Rarely is a book so well positioned to counter these secular lies as this one. The testimony of two women who had every opportunity to pursue worldly womanhood but instead chose biblical womanhood is priceless. You look up from reading the cut-to-the-heart exhortations and inspiring stories, and you can almost see Ruth, Hannah, Mary, and many others calling to a generation of girls, summoning them to defy Satan and seek Christ."

"Every girl has to carve out her own identity in the midst of tempting messages and cultural pressures. Many falter and fail. Kristen and Bethany come to the rescue in *Girl Defined* not only with clear biblical teaching and solid guidance but also with the story of their own personal journeys to God's good design for women."

"*Girl Defined* challenges girls to question 'normal' and think through what will ultimately bring them the most satisfaction in life. (Spoiler alert: it's not necessarily what they've been led to believe!) I appreciate Kristen's and Bethany's courage, vulnerability, and compassion as they start a much-needed conversation about identity."

Jessie Minassian, resident "big sis" at LifeLoveandGod.com
and author of *Crushed*, *Unashamed*, and *Backwards Beauty*

"In a world in which womanhood is increasingly defined by body shape, brand names, boyfriends, bust size, beauty tips, and bawdy sexual mores, someone needs to champion a biblical vision of true beauty—and few do it as well as Kristen and Bethany."

Luke Gilkerson, author of *The Talk: 7 Lessons to Introduce Your Child to Biblical Sexuality*

"In *Girl Defined*, Kristen and Bethany issue a clarion call to every young woman in this generation: cease with the never-ending, never-satisfying attempts to define yourself, and embrace and trust in God's original, good design. Insightful, biblical, and written with passion and conviction, *Girl Defined* encourages girls to choose to be defined by God, resulting in the hope, freedom, purpose, and fulfillment we all long for."

Theresa Wigington Bowen, wife, mother, founder at A Candle in the Window Hospitality Network, and contributor to *Women in the Church*

"Hey, Hollywood, *Vogue*, and MTV . . . what if you are wrong about strong women and sexuality? What if today's girls are looking for beauty that doesn't need a runway? Girls are longing for something deeper than fashion and hair flipping. Kristen and Bethany have answered that call with *Girl Defined*. As a mom and fierce defender of femininity, I am thrilled to get this book into the hands of the women and girls I mentor."

Mona Corwin, author of *Table for Two* and *The Unstoppable Generation*

"Redefining gender is a hot-button issue that parents, church leaders, and counselors must address in our modern culture. *Girl Defined* is a helpful tool for girls and women who are struggling to understand their God-defined femininity. The authors share their personal struggles and offer solutions found in God's Word. Clear analysis of the problem sets the stage for solution-oriented teaching from Scripture. The application section at the end of each chapter makes this a practical study tool for individual or group use. Biblical counselors will find this a helpful resource."

Randy Patten, training director emeritus at the Association of Certified Biblical Counselors and founder of TEAM Focus Ministries

"*Girl Defined* is a book I would have devoured when I was embarking on my own journey of womanhood. I longed to read something written by young women who weren't satisfied with Jesus being an add-on to their culturally comfortable lives. This is that book. Read and find the courage to be a woman who refuses to be defined by anything but God's beautiful design."

GraceAnna Castleberry, pastor's wife and contributor to the Council on Biblical Manhood and Womanhood

"With pertinent illustrations and practical application, Kristen and Bethany have written an excellent book that seeks to encourage women to find their identity, satisfaction, and purpose in Christ alone."

Amanda Peacock, wife, mother, and occasional writer and speaker on biblical womanhood

GIRL
DEFINED

GIRL DEFINED

God's Radical Design for Beauty,
Femininity, and Identity

KRISTEN CLARK AND
BETHANY BAIRD

BakerBooks

a division of Baker Publishing Group
Grand Rapids, Michigan

Published by Baker Books
a division of Baker Publishing Group
P.O. Box 6287, Grand Rapids, MI 49516-6287
www.bakerbooks.com

Printed in the United States of America

Library of Congress Cataloging-in-Publication Data is on file at the Library of Congress, Washington, DC.

ISBN 978-0-8010-0845-0

Unless otherwise indicated, Scripture quotations are from The Holy Bible, English Standard Version® (ESV®), copyright © 2001 by Crossway, a publishing ministry of Good News Publishers. Used by permission. All rights reserved. ESV Text Edition: 2011

Scripture quotations labeled HCSB are from the Holman Christian Standard Bible®, copyright © 1999, 2000, 2002, 2003, 2009 by Holman Bible Publishers. Used by permission. Holman Christian Standard Bible®, Holman CSB®, and HCSB® are federally registered trademarks of Holman Bible Publishers.

Scripture quotations labeled KJV are from the King James Version of the Bible.

Scripture quotations labeled NASB are from the New American Standard Bible®, copyright © 1960, 1962, 1963, 1968, 1971, 1972, 1973, 1975, 1977, 1995 by The Lockman Foundation. Used by permission. (www.Lockman.org)

Scripture quotations labeled NIV are from the Holy Bible, New International Version®. NIV®. Copyright © 1973, 1978, 1984, 2011 by Biblica, Inc.™ Used by permission of Zondervan. All rights reserved worldwide. www.zondervan.com

The names and details of some of the people and situations described in this book have been changed or presented in composite form in order to ensure the privacy of those with whom the authors have worked.

16   17   18   19   20   21   22   7   6   5   4   3   2

To our three younger sisters,
Ellissa, Rebekah, and Suzanna.
May you always be girls defined by God.

CONTENTS

Contents

Part 1

FEMININITY GONE WRONG

1. BULLIED BY THE BIG BAD CHECKLIST

My heart pounded inside my chest. I (Kristen) slowly turned the doorknob on the large glass door. Turning a metal doorknob with sweaty hands is never easy. As the modern office, with its bright white walls and black furniture, came into view, I saw a woman in her early forties with dark brown hair sitting behind a desk. *That must be her*, I thought. She turned in my direction at the sound of the door opening.

"Oh, hey, girl! Come on in," she said with a glossy-lipped smile. "You must be . . . Kristen?" She extended a hand, and I noticed her red nails, flashy bracelets, and blingy rings.

"Yes, thanks so much for having me here today. I really appreciate your time," I replied in a cool tone, trying to conceal my extreme nervousness. The kind of nervousness where you look like a serene beach on the outside but a Category 5 hurricane on the inside. That was me.

"Wow, I think you're the tallest girl I have ever interviewed," she said, her brown eyes looking me up and down. "You might be the perfect fit. Come in and take a seat."

I took a seat in a leather chair across from her desk and crossed my legs. I waited silently for a few seconds (which felt like ten hours) while she shuffled some papers around. My mouth was desert dry at this point. I glanced around the room, wishing I had water.

I took a seat in a white leather chair across from her desk and crossed my legs.

"Okaaay," she finally said, looking up from her desk. "As you know, my name is Jessica Brown, and I'm the owner of this modeling agency. I'm excited about the possibility of having you join our team. Let me explain how things work here . . ."

At that very moment, Bethany was sitting in a similar chair across town being interviewed by a completely different modeling agency.

Bethany's Modeling Interview

"Hi, my name is Jeff. Take a seat, please," he said in a flat tone. I (Bethany) slowly sat down in a plush tan chair.

What a dry personality, I thought to myself. *This is going to be interesting.* I glanced around the office. My eyes were instantly drawn to the image-covered wall behind Jeff. Hundreds of pictures of female models plastered the wall from top to bottom. I scanned the photos and began noticing an unsettling theme. Every model wore an "outfit" a few square inches shy of nudity. Actually, outfit would be a generous term for what these girls were wearing.

"Okay, first fill out this questionnaire and let me know when you're finished," he said, shocking me back to reality.

I took the form and thanked him. My heart started beating a little faster. I wasn't nervous about getting the job anymore. I was nervous about how this interview was going to turn out. Jeff kind of creeped me out. No, he really creeped me out. The last thing I wanted was for my picture to become a new addition to his wallpaper.

I opened the form and quickly scanned the questions on the first page.

"What type of modeling are you most interested in doing?" the opening question asked. My heart picked up the pace as I scanned the options.

A. Swimsuit modeling
B. Lingerie modeling
C. Promo modeling
D. Other

Um . . . is there an option E? With my hands becoming sticky (why does that always happen?), I gripped the pen and went on to the next question.

An Intriguing Road

Believe it or not, becoming models wasn't always a major dream for the two of us. It was more of a vague idea. An intriguing road to try. A glamorous future to imagine. What brought us to these interviews began many years ago with a tiny seed. A thought planted. An idea mentioned. That seed took root and slowly grew in our hearts for many years. Jump back in time with us ten years from this point to see where it all started.

Me, a Glamorous Model?

It was a warm summer afternoon in Texas. (In other words, it was 98 degrees.) I (Kristen) was walking with my mom through an outdoor shopping mall. Tall for my age (twelve at the time) and lanky, I had stringy blonde hair that hung just past my shoulders.

Suddenly, a brunette woman wearing a gray pinstriped suit and pink heels approached us with a big smile.

"Excuse me!" she said. "I saw you two walking by and just had to ask: Does your daughter do any modeling?" This outgoing middle-aged stranger looked at my mom and then locked her gaze on me.

I smiled and gave her a shy no, then glanced at my mom. *A model?* I thought to myself. *At my age?* The woman quickly pulled out a business card from her suit jacket and handed it to my mom.

Believe it or not, becoming models wasn't always a major dream for the two of us.

"Your long legs and blonde hair would make great model material," she said excitedly. She introduced herself and explained that she and her husband worked specifically with young models, ages ten to sixteen, preparing them for a career in the industry. They owned a large house in Dallas, and many of their young modeling recruits lived with them. She told us that her models worked for the biggest agencies in Dallas and were on their way to becoming top models.

"They also get paid really well," she said, taking a more serious tone.

She asked my mom if we would be interested in coming to her house to look into the opportunity. She even offered a bedroom for me and said I could live at their house if I was interested! I could tell my mom was slightly shocked and flattered by her offer. In the end, my mom kindly declined, explaining that a modeling career wasn't what she or my dad had in mind for my future.

"At least talk to your husband and think about it some more," the lady urged.

"We'll think about it," my mom said and smiled. We thanked her and walked away to continue our shopping.

I had never thought of myself as a model until then. A *real* model? A *beautiful* model? A seed of curiosity took root in my heart that day. For the first time I wondered what the life of a glamorous model would be like.

Helmet Head and Barrette Babe

While Kristen was imagining life as a model someday, I (Bethany) was still very much immersed in being a kid. I was sweet and innocent and couldn't have cared less about looking "pretty." Even though I'm only a year and a half younger than Kristen, I wasn't as interested in growing up quickly.

With short, frizzy hair, a partial unibrow, huge glasses, and missing teeth, I'll be the first to admit that I was not much to look at. If someone had told me then that I would interview for a modeling job someday, I would have given them my famous cross-eyed look.

It wasn't until Kristen began paying more attention to her clothes and hair that I became curious about beauty as well. Little sisters want to be like their big sisters. Although Kristen's newfound interest in looking pretty was getting stronger, she didn't quite know how to put it into action yet. Brushing her hair into a super tight ponytail, then dousing her head with hairspray was her version of a fashionable look. In fact, she doused her head with so much hairspray that she acquired the flattering nickname "Helmet Head." Our family still jokes about her helmet-head look.

For the first time I wondered what the life of a "glamorous" model would be like.

As the months went by, I finally developed my own interest in beauty and decided to try a few "fashion" looks of my own. One day before church, I opened up a pack of metal hair barrettes. Instead of using one, two, or even three, I thought it would be cool to put the entire pack in my hair. After securing a tight ponytail (no hairspray for me), I lined both sides of my head with dozens of shimmering barrettes (hence the reason I didn't need hairspray). If only you could have seen the look of satisfaction on my face. Oh yeah. Barrette babe coming through! I headed out the door thinking I was the hottest chick on the planet.

Looking back on our childhood always makes me and Kristen laugh. You probably laugh at yours too. We thought we were totally cool and hip when it came to our fashion choices. Although we were young and fashion illiterate, something was changing in us. Our desire to be beautiful and valued by the people around us began to form. We began noticing the beautiful faces on billboards. The sensual women on magazine covers. The perfect hair on shampoo commercials. The bone-thin models on mall posters. We noticed these things—and we liked them. These images appealed to our inner desire to be beautiful. To be feminine. To be women.

Our desire to be beautiful and valued by the people around us began to form.

The prevailing secular culture enticed us with its version of femininity. Its perception of romance. Its idea of family. Its explanation of success.

Little by little the subtle undertow of our culture's ideology shaped our views of womanhood.

Am I as Pretty as Sally?

Do you remember how old you were when you started to care about being pretty?

As little girls, it seems like the first insecurity we pick up revolves around our looks. Then we grow a little older and worry about our talents. Then our jobs. Then our husbands. Then our kids. Then our houses. Then our success. Overall, our worth.

We're constantly asking ourselves if we're good enough, if we have all the right ducks in the right rows. What started out as a simple *Am I as pretty as Sally?* when we were twelve turns into an identity crisis when we're thirty.

From the time we were little girls until now, our culture has been feeding us messages of what womanhood is all about. We each took note of what sounded good to us. We internalized a running identity checklist. *Oh, that's what womanhood is about? Got it. Check. Oh, I'm supposed to be that skinny? Got it. Check. Oh, I'm supposed to have a successful career? Got it. Check. Oh, I'm supposed to get married when I'm young . . . older . . . never? Um, got it. Check. I think.*

From the first moment a woman questions her identity, she begins wondering about her womanhood and whether she measures up. Our big bad identity checklist is always growing. But what makes things even more complicated is that the rules are always changing. One year our culture strongly encourages us to get married by a certain age. Then five years later the age has changed! One year we are considered successful if we graduate with an undergrad degree. Then several years later we need a master's degree to be deemed truly successful. One year culture says we should have babies younger. Then five years later we're supposed to wait until we're older—or skip having babies altogether.

> *From the first moment a woman questions her identity, she begins wondering about her womanhood and whether she measures up.*

The list is endless. When are we, as women, good enough? What does it take to become a "complete" woman? What is true femininity supposed to look like? What does it mean to be successful? How pretty is pretty enough? Are happiness and fulfillment a reality or only a dream?

Millions of women just like you, just like us, have been asking these same questions for a long time. We've tried everything we know how to do, but it isn't working. We're not satisfied. We're not happy. We're not peaceful. The results of this endless searching are devastating. The two of us have seen it ruin girls and women over and over again. Is this all there is for women? Is what we see as good as it gets?

In short, absolutely not. No way. Our culture's version of womanhood is a far (and we mean far) cry from who God designed us to be. He has something radically better for womanhood. Something much more fulfilling than a checklist. We'll unpack what that means in the pages to come.

Why We Wrote This Book

Instead of offering you a new beauty cream, a better career choice, a higher form of education, or a handsome prince on a white horse, we want to recommend something better. Something you won't find in the culture. We're here to throw a flag on the field of modern femininity and say, "Enough is enough." It's not working. It's time to try something different.

The reason we wrote this book is to give you a radically better vision for what true womanhood is all about. The only hope we have as women is to stop defining ourselves according to other people's standards and start defining it according to God's Word. In order to become all God created you to be, you have to gain a vision for what true God-defined femininity is all about.

As Elisabeth Elliot says so well,

> We are called to be women. The fact that I am a woman does not make me a different kind of Christian, but the fact that I am a Christian does make me a different kind of woman. For I have accepted God's idea for me, and my whole life is an offering back to Him of all that I am and all that He wants me to be.[1]

We don't claim to have all the answers, but we do have some. God has shown us incredible, life-changing truths about womanhood that we cannot keep to ourselves. The results of following God's design far outweigh the results culture has ever promoted.

As a result of following God's plan, we can honestly say we are each happier, more fulfilled, and more content than we have ever been in our lives. God's Word is true, and his version of womanhood offers lasting results.

Throughout the pages of this book, you will discover

- why God created the female gender,
- what your purpose is as a woman,
- how to obtain lasting worth,
- what true beauty looks like,
- how to apply femininity to your romantic relationships,
- what God's idea of a working woman looks like, and
- how to leave behind a lasting legacy that doesn't fade with time.

God is looking for women like you to courageously go against the grain of modern culture. He needs women who are brave. Women who will set a new trend, think outside the box, and raise the bar for femininity. He needs women who refuse to live for the applause of this world and instead live for the applause of their King.

Susan Hunt, a godly woman and author says, "It is time for women of biblical faith to reclaim our territory. We know the Designer. We have His instruction manual. If we don't display the Divine design of His female creation, no one will. But if we do, it will be a profound testimony to a watching, needy world."[2]

God's Word is true, and his version of womanhood offers lasting results.

No matter how old you are or what season of life you're in, if you're a woman, this book is for you. Your story is far from complete. Our stories are far from complete. Not many women have the courage to put down the pen for their big bad identity checklist. But those who do have discovered something remarkable. Something life transforming.

You'll meet some of these women throughout this book. They stopped allowing the culture to define their womanhood. They stood up to the big bad bully of counterfeit femininity and said, "No more!"

Instead, they've chosen to become girls defined by God. The results are astounding. We've tried it. And it's undoubtedly worth it.

Watch out though. Radical things happen when God gets ahold of your checklist.

CHAPTER 1
STUDY GUIDE

Stop defining your femininity according to the culture, and start defining it according to God's Word.

1. How old were you when you started to care about being pretty? What prompted you to start caring?

   _____

   _____

   _____

2. Every woman has a big bad checklist. Check all the boxes that apply to you: *I have sought to find my identity and worth through . . .*

   ☐ Being perfectly skinny

   ☐ Having a pretty face

   ☐ Maintaining a successful career

   ☐ Keeping a boyfriend

   ☐ Getting married

   ☐ Being independent

   ☐ Owning nice things

   ☐ Wearing the latest trends

   ☐ Traveling to nice places

   ☐ Being athletic

☐ Accomplishing academic goals

☐ Gathering many friends

☐ Other _____

☐ Other _____

How many boxes did you check? Why are you seeking to find your identity in those things?

3. What are your biggest insecurities right now?

_____

_____

_____

4. What do you think will bring you lasting worth and satisfaction?

_____

_____

_____

5. Name three things you are hoping to learn by reading this book:

_____

_____

_____

MAKE IT HAPPEN *Today*

To start things off, take a moment right now to pray and ask God to help you get the most out of this book.

PS: We're excited you're reading it!

2. BLONDE BOMBSHELLS DON'T HAVE WHAT IT TAKES

She starred in thirty major films. She was awarded a Golden Globe for "Female World Film Favorite." She started her own production company. She was voted "2nd Greatest Movie Star" of all time by *Premiere* magazine. She was chosen by *Empire* magazine as one of the "100 Sexiest Stars in Film History." She was beautiful, talented, and successful and seemed to have everything a woman could dream of . . . except for one thing. Happiness.

Norma Jeane Baker, the third child of Gladys Pearl Baker, was born in a Los Angeles county hospital on June 1, 1926. She didn't know who her real dad was and had no father figure in her life. Her mom, who had been diagnosed as mentally unstable, was incapable of caring for the young Norma Jeane. So Gladys placed her in a foster home where she lived until she was seven. In 1933, Gladys bought a house and brought Norma Jeane back to live with her.

Only a few months after moving in, her mother started having mental breakdowns again and was institutionalized at the state mental hospital. Norma Jeane was scared, confused, and alone.

She spent the rest of her childhood bouncing from foster homes to orphanages. She was reported to have been sexually abused on several occasions during her childhood. Her life was the epitome of dysfunction.

To escape the constant rotation of foster homes and orphanages, she married a man named Jim Dougherty at the young age of sixteen. She was intrigued by the Hollywood scene and decided to apply at the Blue Book Model Agency. She was told they were looking for blonde models, so she quickly bleached her brunette hair platinum blonde.

She became one of the Blue Book's most successful models, appearing on dozens of magazine covers. Her career took flight. She was quickly noticed by the film industry and began acting and singing. Norma Jeane became very successful and was well known by everyone.

As time went on, her career, as well as her personal life, began experiencing some major ups and downs. She was married and divorced three times and had many affairs in between. Her physical and mental health began to decline as she struggled with drug addiction and insomnia. Her life was a huge mess.

The public loved what she gave them, but she knew they didn't truly love her as a person. Her makeup-covered face, dyed blonde hair, and sparkling clothes only hid what she was feeling on the inside. Depressed. Unloved. Alone. Sadly, the beauty and fame wasn't enough to satisfy Norma Jeane. She committed suicide at the young age of thirty-six. Before she died she said:

> I knew I belonged to the public and to the world, not because I was talented or even beautiful, but because I had never belonged to anything or anyone else.
>
> Marilyn Monroe

Norma Jeane Baker changed her name to Marilyn Monroe in 1947. The world doesn't like to acknowledge the dark side of her story. The only Marilyn we see is the happy-go-lucky bombshell on posters at the mall. She's usually smiling. Looks happy. Looks fulfilled.

Sadly, the beauty and fame weren't enough to satisfy Norma Jeane. She committed suicide at the young age of thirty-six.

Marilyn is portrayed as the all-American "dream girl." She's an icon millions of girls and women look up to. However, her short life is a tragic example of one woman's endless search for identity. The more she searched for happiness, the longer her checklist became. If one thing didn't work, she tried something new. Beauty. Fame. Money. Marriage. Sex. Drugs. Popularity. You name it, she tried it. Marilyn's entire life was driven by what she thought would bring her fulfillment as a woman. She's the epitome of a girl defined by her culture. And she suffered greatly as a result.

Marilyn's life story brings up some serious questions. It challenges culture's assumptions about the superficial things that are "supposed" to make a person feel happy and fulfilled. For instance:

- How could a woman who had "everything" still feel unfulfilled?
- If being famous leads to happiness, then why didn't it work for Marilyn?
- If being drop-dead gorgeous brings contentment, then why was Marilyn depressed?
- If having a successful career brings security, then why did Marilyn struggle regularly with insomnia?
- If wealth brings freedom, then why did Marilyn commit suicide?

It's obvious that something wasn't working. Something wasn't right.

Where did Marilyn's life take its first wrong turn? It most likely happened where many of us take our first wrong turn. It all started the moment she allowed the culture to define her womanhood. The moment the culture's ideas filled her checklist. The moment God's design for femininity was dismissed from her vocabulary. So what role did the definition of womanhood according to the culture play in Marilyn's tragic life? No doubt, it was a huge one. Her unmatched physical beauty and larger-than-life personality made her the world's number one sex symbol, but being in the top spot in the public's eye could not fix the inner struggles she faced. Like many of us, she probably thought the next checkbox would do it. *This will be it. I'll finally be happy now.* But happiness remained elusive.

How could a woman who had "everything" still feel unfulfilled?

Sadly, the lies Marilyn believed are still alive and well today. They're just packaged a little differently now. And they're being shoved down our throats quicker than we can swallow.

Dropping Off the Radar

Unlike Marilyn, the two of us grew up in a Christian family with involved parents. Softball. Basketball. Swimming. Piano. Guitar. Gymnastics. Awana. Ballet. We did it all. And our parents, along with our six siblings (Michael, Stephen, Ellissa, Timothy, Rebekah, and Suzanna), were right there cheering us on. Being homeschooled also brought our large family closer together.

As we entered our teen years and began venturing farther from the nest of home, our parents became cautious about the friends we hung out with. They intentionally got us involved in church activities so we would be surrounded by godly influences. Between homeschooling, playing basketball, working at a Christian bookstore, and being heavily involved at our church, we were busy girls.

Deep friendships formed, and we slowly developed our core group of close friends. These were our go-to people. Our best friends. We loved these girls. Then we had our semi-core group of friends. These were the people we hung out with here and there but not on a regular basis. Then we had our casual group. These were the people we didn't really hang out with unless a social event united us. You know what we're talking about.

All "friends" considered, we grew up in a group of around thirty Christian girls. Each of these girls came from Christian homes. Each of these girls claimed to love Jesus. They desired to honor God with their lives. They each believed in things like purity, saving sex until marriage, and dressing with decency. We loved having so many like-minded friends.

As high school came to a close, our roads began to part. Some stayed local like us. Others ventured far away. Distance wasn't a huge problem though. We still kept in touch.

We never would have predicted what came next. Over the next five years, strange things started happening. One by one our friends dropped off the radar. And we don't mean the "staying in touch radar." We're talking about the Christian radar.

We never would have predicted what came next.

We watched some of our godliest friends turn into complete atheists. We saw other friends reject purity and dive headfirst into sexual relationships. Some got married and then quickly divorced. A couple of single friends got pregnant out of wedlock. We also witnessed quiet friends turn into raunchy party animals.

As the years went on, many of our friends continued dropping off the Christian radar. They no longer embraced biblical femininity (we'll dive into what that looks like later). Instead, they slowly transformed into culture-defined girls.

Sadly, the passion for God they had in high school became extinct from their lives. They no longer talked, acted, or looked like Christian girls. Their lives didn't reflect the joy, peace, order, purity, and holiness of God. From that large group of thirty, we can count on one hand the girls who are still walking with God. The girls who still care about biblical values. The girls who still use the Bible as their standard for truth.

This shocking epidemic deeply concerns us. What happened to our friends? What went wrong? Why did so many jump ship?

Some people blame it on poor choices. And yes, poor choices do have consequences. But we think it's much deeper than that. The more we studied biblical womanhood, the clearer the answer became.

Freedom Doesn't Travel Solo

When people graduate from high school, they enter a new world of adulthood. They have to make big decisions about the next step in their lives. As the two of us and our friends entered this new phase of responsibility, we also entered a new world of freedom. We had the freedom to make more decisions. To think for ourselves. To decide what we wanted to do with our time.

This newfound freedom didn't travel solo though. It was accompanied by a sly new group of temptations. Our identity wasn't as complicated when we were young girls. Now we had a million different decisions, ideas, and opportunities in front of us. Oh yes, the identity checklist was there in high school. But it was nothing like what we faced as young adults.

As we each traveled down different paths, the identity checklist followed us. The culture's version of womanhood began softly whispering in our ears. "Sex before marriage isn't really that bad . . . Come on, have a little fun." "Just have a few more drinks. You'll like getting drunk." "Don't be so stiff about your clothes—loosen up a little. Embrace your seductive side." "Getting married is a thing of the past. There's no harm in living with your boyfriend." "The Bible was written two thousand years ago. Be a little more progressive."

Our personal views of God and his standards were being challenged—on every front. Every corner we turned, the world was tugging on us to join in. And it looked fun. It looked exciting. It looked fulfilling. The same lies that enticed Marilyn Monroe were enticing us. And they were relentless.

The culture's version of womanhood began softly whispering in our ears.

One by one many of our friends bought into the alluring lies. They wanted something new. Something more. Little by little they stopped looking to God for their identity. They stopped asking him what he thought. They stopped believing his truths.

Ultimately, it wasn't their wrong decisions that led them down that road. It was their wrong thinking. It started the first time they questioned God's Word. It started the first time they believed a small lie. It started the first time they allowed culture to define their identity. It started the first time they looked to something other than God for their happiness. Anyone could wind up sliding down this slippery slope.

Although we never jumped ship, our journey hasn't been without some bumps. We've been tempted, and we've failed. We've been lured, and we've given in. We've bought into the lies. We've allowed the culture to define us at times. And we're ashamed of it. But we've never thrown in the towel. We're still holding on to God's Word with all our might. We're clinging to his truths. We're still trusting that his plan for our womanhood is better than Hollywood's.

C. S. Lewis says, "God can't give us peace and happiness apart from himself because there is no such thing."[1] Apart from God, lasting peace and happiness do not exist. That is why Marilyn's search never ended. That is why her identity checklist never stopped growing. And sadly, the same thing is happening to many Christian women today.

Katie Jones, a girl we both knew in high school, learned this lesson the hard way. Instead of looking to Christ for her identity, she chose the path of counterfeit femininity. In the next chapter, we'll take a peek at her story and try to understand why this alluring version of womanhood has cracks in its foundation.

Apart from God, lasting peace and happiness do not exist.

CHAPTER 2

STUDY GUIDE

STASH IT IN YOUR HEART

The moment we allow culture to define our womanhood is the moment we take our first wrong turn.

1. What stands out to you about Marilyn Monroe's life?

   _____

   _____

   _____

2. Why do you think Marilyn, a woman who had "everything," still felt unfulfilled?

   _____

   _____

   _____

3. In what ways is today's culture whispering lies into our ears? Circle all that you've been tempted to believe:

   "Sex before marriage isn't really that bad . . . Come on, have a little fun."

   "Just have a few more drinks. You'll like getting drunk."

   "Don't be so stiff about your clothes—loosen up a little. Embrace your seductive side."

"Getting married is a thing of the past. There's no harm in living with your boyfriend."

"The Bible was written two thousand years ago. Be a little more progressive."

4. Have you, or someone you know, ever jumped ship? Why?

_____

_____

_____

5. Pull out your Bible and look up Romans 12:2. How can this verse help you avoid an outcome like Marilyn's?

_____

_____

_____

MAKE IT HAPPEN *Today*

Read Romans 12:2 again. Spend a few minutes memorizing this verse.

3. COUNTERFEIT FEMININITY, YOU'VE DONE ME WRONG

I (Kristen) recognized Katie Jones the moment she walked through the door. All eyes in the summer camp gym gradually turned in her direction as she walked to her seat. Her legs were long. Her heels were high. Her hair was Pantene Pro-V come to life. Her lips were shimmering. Her jeans were tight. Her midriff was her trademark. The way she walked screamed, "I am confident!"

I watched as she turned her head and flipped her hair so perfectly it was commercial worthy. She waved to a group of guys, giving them her pearly white smile. I took note of how the guys smiled and talked to one another after she walked by. This girl was the real deal. She was living up to the "Wow! She is amazing" rumors I had heard about her.

I wouldn't have said it out loud, but I was jealous of her. I wanted to have what she had. The confidence. The independence. The beauty. The sexy body. I described her in the same way a guy says, "He's the man," only I said, "She's the woman."

Over the next few years, I watched Katie stay on the cutting edge of modern womanhood. She was always the first to test the new fashion trends. She was always the first to push the limits. From my perspective, Katie seemed to be totally in control of her life.

Fast forward ten years to now. Katie is still very independent. She still appears confident. She's still on top of all the fashion trends. To the public eye she looks put together, but behind the scenes she's falling apart.

To the public eye she looks put together, but behind the scenes she's falling apart.

Katie married her high school sweetheart in the midst of pursuing her college degree. Less than one year into her marriage, Katie regretted her decision. Settling into married life with a husband attempting to "lead" her wasn't quite what she had expected. As the second year of marriage rolled around, Katie shocked us all. She left her husband and demanded a divorce.

Shortly after her divorce, Katie entered the party scene. She quickly found a new man who was enamored by her independent spirit and sexy outfits. The last time I saw Katie Jones she was eight months pregnant, working as a full-time waitress, partying on the weekends, and living with the boyfriend who got her pregnant.

Watching Katie over the years felt like a front-row seat to a celebrity's life. She was the most popular girl in town. She was the girl everyone was jealous of in high school. She was the girl who appeared to have it all. She was the woman. And now her life is filled with dysfunction and heartache. Her popularity is gone. Her friends have moved on. She's no longer the girl people look up to. Despite everything she had going for her, it clearly wasn't enough.

Aiming at the Bull's-Eye

The last time Bethany and I went to the grocery store, I noticed something. Every magazine cover was filled with images of beautiful, confident, fashionable, and sexy women who reminded me of Katie Jones. The women on these magazine covers are portrayed as having it all. If I thought Katie Jones was the woman, these women easily surpass her.

They star in the most popular TV shows. They sing hit songs. They've divorced the "hottest" men on earth and appear to be happy about their decisions. They are the role models for all of womanhood, and they are leading us into the future of femininity.

One magazine cover featured an insanely popular reality star. She wore a plunging white tank top, and the magazine was plastered with the words "Look Sexy Now. Make Them Obsessed with You."

Modern femininity, according to celebrity idols, is all about looking sexy, exuding confidence, and remaining independent of men.

Another magazine featured a famous pop singer. She was wearing a micro-miniskirt and a shirt that barely covered the essential areas. The bold words read, "Why Your Last Breakup Was Awesome."

The last magazine pictured an actress wearing a black formal gown with a slit past her thigh. Large words read, "Wake Up Hotter. Sleepy to Sexy in 5 Minutes Flat."

I got the hint. Modern femininity, according to celebrity idols, is all about looking sexy, exuding confidence, and remaining independent of men. If we follow in their footsteps, we'll find the happiness and fulfillment we desire. Right?

After looking over such magazines, it becomes clear that every woman is after the same thing. We all want happiness. We all want fulfillment. We all want security. We all want to feel loved.

The problem is getting there. How do we, as women, obtain these things?

As Bethany and I talked about this, we realized that femininity is like a target. The bull's-eye is in the middle surrounded by various rings. It contains everything we want. Confidence. Security. Peace. Fulfillment. Joy. Love. Satisfaction. In order to hit the bull's-eye, we, as women, need to use the correct bow and arrows. We can't hit the bull's-eye if we're using the wrong tools. We will try and fail every time.

Each of us desperately wants to use the right tools to shoot our arrows. We want to hit the bull's-eye of true femininity and obtain the fulfillment we desire. Ultimately, the bull's-eye leads to true satisfaction, and everything else leads to endless pursuits.

Katie Jones was missing the bull's-eye. Sadly, her life was built on the ideas of counterfeit femininity. She followed her favorite celebrities and shot her arrows in the direction they suggested. Her results were anything but glamorous.

Three Pillars of Counterfeit Femininity

Katie Jones adopted what the two of us call the "Three Pillars of Counterfeit Femininity." These three pillars are the core of our culture's version of femininity. They are the must-haves for women of the twenty-first century.

Have you ever evaluated your life and asked yourself why you do what you do?

It's easy to look at Katie and think, *Well, I'm not as bad as she is. I haven't embraced culture's ideas like she has. I'm way better off.* Maybe you are better off than Katie. Maybe you haven't fully welcomed counterfeit femininity like she did. But have you ever stopped to check? Have you ever evaluated your life and asked yourself why you do what you do? Why do you believe what you believe?

When the two of us asked ourselves these questions several years back, we each realized that many of our actions and beliefs were a direct result of our culture's influence. In fact, we could tell you many stories of ways in which we accepted the Three Pillars of Counterfeit Femininity. We used the wrong arrows and aimed in the wrong direction. Here are a few of those stories.

PILLAR #1: LIBERATION

I (Bethany) remember this conversation like it was yesterday. I was twenty-two years old. Gutsy and fierce. I was convinced that it was my way or the highway. I hate to admit this, but I was a bit of a know-it-all. I hadn't quite learned the meaning of tact. If I thought I was right, I wanted to make sure the other person knew it.

One day I encountered a major disagreement with one of my guy friends. Not pretty. Here's what went down.

My friend Brandon and I were hanging out with a group of friends at a local coffee shop. It was a sunny Saturday afternoon, and we were attempting to have a fun, enjoyable time. Somehow, someway, a conversation started that hit me in every wrong spot.

Brandon and I got on the topic of my current ministry projects and goals. I was very into my ministry projects. They were my pride and joy. I had convinced myself that my ministry accomplishments were the source of my purpose and fulfillment as a woman. I looked around at married women and thought, *I can't imagine being just a wife and mother. I can't imagine not having something else. Not accomplishing something bigger. Something better.* I didn't say that out loud, but I thought it in my head. I felt it in my heart.

Now imagine what happened when Brandon asked me, "Do you think you could be happy as a wife and mother? Would you be willing to give up some of your ministry projects in the future if you needed to?"

Wow! Not a cool question. I spun around in my swivel chair, looked him in the eyes, and, in my feistiest tone said, "I really can't imagine my life without my ministry and book projects. I hope that whoever I marry will be supportive of my unique gifts and talents."

As you can imagine, the conversation didn't end there. Brandon's question caused me to do some serious thinking. I waded through questions like, *Why am I so defensive of my accomplishments? Why do I feel the need to prove myself to those around me? Why do I feel being a wife and mother isn't good enough? Why do I feel so restless and discontent?*

After several weeks of soul-searching, I realized the truth. My ministry wasn't the problem. Brandon wasn't the problem. My job wasn't the problem. My goals weren't the problem. It was my heart.

Somewhere along the way, I had come to accept aspects of the first pillar of counterfeit femininity: *liberation.*

Liberation has one underlying theme: to throw off the "old-fashioned" idea that men and women have differing roles and unique purposes. Liberation is about women being free. Free from what? Primarily free from roles in marriage. Free from the differences between men and women. Free from the Bible's teachings on gender. Free from anything that distinguishes what it means to be male and what it means to be female. One dictionary defines the word liberation as "the removal of traditional social or sexual rules, attitudes, etc."[1] We translate that to mean "out with the old, in with the new." This is the twenty-first century. Women shouldn't be tied down to traditional views.

Liberation pushes the idea that to be equal with men, women need to have the same purpose as men. We need to accomplish

> *Liberation pushes the idea that to be equal with men, women need to have the same purpose as men.*

the same things. We need to pursue the same lifestyle. Only then, when the gender lines are merged, will we be truly satisfied.

In my heart, I had come to believe that my worth was found in my accomplishments outside of my home and family. I thought, *Being a wife and mother is okay, but real women are doing more. They're getting jobs. Running big ministries. Traveling. Proving they can do just as much as—if not more than—men.*

I wasn't blind to our culture's accolades. The women who were ditching the "old-fashioned" roles of being a wife and mother were the ones getting the applause. The women who were getting the jobs and pursuing careers were considered successful.

I was no dummy. I wanted to be accepted by the culture. I wanted to be praised. As a result, I pursued opportunities that would get me the applause I was craving.

"Oh, you are writing a book? Impressive."

"You run a blog for young women? Incredible."

"How many young women do you mentor? Wow! Amazing."

"You're the director of that program? Cool."

The crazy thing was that the praise didn't make me happy. In fact, I was quite frustrated. I was on edge. I was ready to prove my worth to those around me. I acted high and mighty toward men. I was an unhappy mess packaged in spiritual wrapping paper.

I was an unhappy mess packaged in spiritual wrapping paper.

The conversation I had with Brandon caused me to do some serious soul-searching. It made me humble myself and evaluate my heart. It was then that I realized I wasn't shooting at the right target. I wasn't aiming my arrows at God's bull's-eye. I was aiming at counterfeit femininity. I was trying to prove my worth as a woman. I was embracing aspects of liberation.

Lightbulb moment!

No wonder I felt so dissatisfied. No wonder I was restless. No wonder I was fierce and feisty. No wonder I was like a cannon ready to shoot when Brandon asked me that question. I was on the wrong path. Shooting at the wrong target.

Like many of you, I was hoping to find fulfillment in a lifestyle liberated from God's design for the woman (which we will discuss in more detail later).

PILLAR #2: INDEPENDENCE

Growing up, I (Kristen) was the epitome of the word *competitive*. I've always had this burning fire inside of me to win. It doesn't matter what the activity is.

A while back I discovered I have this weird ability to wiggle my tongue up and down in my mouth at lightning speeds. It's strange, I know. I don't know who in their right mind but me would care about challenging someone to a game of who-can-wiggle-their-tongue-up-and-down-the-fastest. For some reason I find this challenge thrilling. I give you permission to pause your reading and try it. Who knows? Maybe you have a skill you never knew about.

The truth is I am still very competitive. Sometimes my younger sisters, Ellissa and Rebekah, have to remind me that "it's just a game. There's no point in creating enemies over it." Ahhh . . . wisdom from the younger sisters.

As I grew into a woman, my competitive attitude started to morph into something different. Something more distinct. Something that became very apparent as I began my relationship with Zack (who is now my husband). It was an attitude of independence. An attitude of *I've got this. I don't need you.*

I took pride in my ability to fend for myself. I was a capable woman. I didn't need a man's help—especially if that man tried to tell me what to do. It's not that I hated men, because I didn't.

I actually really liked them. I was pro-marriage, pro-family, pro all that stuff.

So what was this feeling inside of me? Why did I cringe at the idea of giving up control? Of releasing my independence? Of needing others? Of accepting help? Of needing advice?

As I entered my marriage with Zack, I slowly began to adopt the second pillar of counterfeit femininity: *independence.* I was living out the culture's definition of a strong woman. I looked around and imitated what I saw. I took note of what I heard. I unknowingly adopted the mind-set of women who were portrayed as strong and successful.

I took pride in my ability to fend for myself. I was a capable woman.

Early in my marriage my independent spirit reared its ugly head on a regular basis. I remember one specific time when Zack and I had been married for only six months. We were living in an adorable one-bedroom apartment, sharing the same car, and following the same budget. It seemed romantic and sweet at first to share everything.

Zack and I both agreed that he would be in charge of managing our family budget (I can't stand managing budgets). He came up with a plan and showed it to me. I was pleasantly surprised when he allotted me a generous amount of spending money and gladly accepted.

Well, several weeks later he realized that our budget was out of balance, and we would both need to cut back on our spending money. Oh boy. That didn't go over well with me.

"Wait . . . I can only spend how much?" I asked in a defiant tone.

"Look, babe, I'm really sorry. I would give you all the money in the world if I could," he replied calmly. "We just don't have it in our budget right now."

I gave him a cold stare.

"Well, how am I supposed to buy what I need? I don't want to be so restricted and tied down," I said holding one hand in the air.

The whole idea of sharing everything didn't seem so romantic anymore. I wanted the freedom to do what I wanted, when I wanted. In that moment, being independent seemed a lot more appealing to me.

This whole budget conflict turned into a two-day conversation. It caused us to have some much-needed deep conversations. Like Bethany, I did some serious soul-searching of my own during this time. I had no idea how independent my spirit was until I was put to the test.

I was buying into pillar #2 far more than I had ever realized. In our modern culture, an independent woman is considered highly successful, powerful, and strong. I knew this and subconsciously bought into the message.

In that moment, being independent seemed a lot more appealing to me.

Instead of viewing Zack as my teammate, I viewed him as my competition and pushed against him.

Have you ever ridden in a canoe with someone? If so, you know that both people have to work as a team to get to their destination. If one person decides to independently paddle in their own direction, the canoe will spin in circles.

This is exactly what my independent attitude did to my marriage. The more I embraced that mind-set, the more my marriage spun in circles. Having a self-sufficient attitude left me with a weak and strained relationship. It left me feeling defensive toward Zack. It left me with a chip on my shoulder and a desire to prove myself. Pursuing independence was stressful and unfulfilling.

Instead of spinning my canoe in circles, I've since decided to use my strength to paddle against the current of modern independence. I've redirected my arrows at the correct target and am now aiming for the bull's-eye. Honestly, I'm amazed at how much more peace and purpose I now feel. I view my marriage in a completely different light. Zack is now my teammate, not my competitor.

Whether you're currently married or single, our culture is pressuring you to attain an unhealthy level of independence. You're encouraged to separate yourself from your parents, from your family, from your husband, and from your children. You're encouraged to pursue what you want, when you want it. "Shove everyone aside because you come first."

God designed us to function best when we're paddling together for a cause greater than ourselves.

However, this lifestyle is not what God intended for us as women. God designed us to function best when we're paddling together for a cause greater than ourselves. In the chapters to come, we'll unpack exactly what that looks like.

PILLAR #3: SEXUAL FREEDOM

The two of us weren't trained. We weren't taught. We just knew. We doubled up the mascara, slathered on the lip gloss, and posed for the camera. Eyes with a look of longing, lips slightly puckered, and fingers gently tugging on a few strands of hair.

The wind blew perfectly. Our photographer snapped the pictures. In our minds we were on top of the Eiffel Tower modeling for the cover of a famous magazine. Our adoring fans would be waiting at the bottom of the tower hoping to catch a glimpse of us or maybe, if they were lucky, an autograph.

Reality check!

I (Bethany) hate to admit this, but we were a far cry from the Eiffel Tower. Or the Leaning Tower of Pisa. Or any tower. We were actually on top of our roof, in our backyard, with our little sister

(Ellissa) snapping pictures. Our biggest fan was the stinky dog hoping to snatch a treat from us on our way down the rickety ladder.

Looking back, we can't help but laugh at what our neighbors must have thought. Two tall blondes, decked out in bling, attempting to pose like world-famous models while taking photos on the roof of their own house. I'm sure we were some kind of interesting sight.

In that moment on the roof, we wouldn't have used the word *seductive* to describe ourselves or our poses, but that's exactly what we were going for. We weren't blind. We saw the women on the magazines. We knew they were chosen for a reason. We knew if we copied their poses and showed off our pictures (via social media), we would get the attention and affirmation we wanted.

> We imitated the famous women in the spotlight in hopes of finding the security and value we longed for.

At this point in time, the two of us were teenage girls, and pillar #3—sexual freedom—was already hitting us with a mighty force. Even as Christian girls growing up in a Christian family with awesome Christian parents, the pressure to be sexually loose was intense. We wanted to be liked and accepted. We wanted to be "beautiful." We imitated the famous women in the spotlight in hopes of finding the security and value we longed for.

Fast forward a few years to when the two of us were in our early twenties standing at the soda fountain in a local restaurant and a totally random lady walked up to us.

"Excuse me. I just had to come up and tell you girls how much I love your height. Are you models?"

"Oh, you're so sweet," I (Bethany) replied. "But no, we aren't models."

"What a shame," she said, shaking her head. "Well, let me offer you two girls some advice. Don't let those bodies go to waste. Seriously. Use it and own it!"

"Oh. Okay . . . thanks," I replied, glancing at Kristen.

The pressure to use our sexual freedom had hit us again.

Thankfully, we'd matured quite a bit since our rooftop photo shoot. We had studied God's design for our sexuality and knew better. We still felt the pressure to conform to culture's idea of beauty and sexual freedom, but we weren't as easily swayed.

After that lady left, the two of us talked about what she said. We agreed that being a woman in today's sex-saturated culture is hard. We definitely didn't need the added pressure from a random stranger telling us to basically "flaunt what we've got."

Fast forward another year.

The two of us were drinking coffee with a group of girlfriends. Summer was just around the corner, which meant bathing suit season was upon us. In a roundabout sort of way, one of our friends asked if the two of us wore bikinis. I (Bethany) kindly explained to our friend that Kristen and I had chosen not to do the bikini thing as a result of our personal convictions on modesty. Our friend was not satisfied with my answer. In fact, she seemed very offended by it. She took it upon herself to lecture us on why we should wear bikinis and why we should feel totally comfortable showing off our bodies. She explained that exposing our skin was a sign of confidence and security.

Once again, society's idea of sexual freedom was being shoved in our faces.

As teens we were pressured by the media to live up to a sexualized version of womanhood. As young women we were pressured to use our freedom and flaunt our bodies. "Don't let them go to waste" was a stranger's advice.

Now as grown women we were being told that showing off our bodies was a sign of security and confidence. Real women aren't ashamed of their bodies. Real women are confident in showing it all. Real women value their sexual freedom.

Maybe you can relate to some of what we've said. Maybe you can't. Maybe you've never stopped to consider what we're talking about. No matter your age, stage, or experiences in life, the bottom line is this: we live in a sex-saturated culture. It's impossible to completely avoid it. We are bombarded with misguided messages of sexual freedom while performing some of the most basic activities in life—like going to a grocery or clothing store.

The third pillar, *sexual freedom*, pushes women toward one thing: proving their worth with their bodies. Counterfeit femininity says that real women are sexy, hot, free, edgy, and wild.

The two of us have a question though. If that's what makes a "real" woman, why are so many sexually free women struggling? Why did the sex icon Marilyn Monroe commit suicide if she had everything the culture says makes a real woman? Why did Miranda Kerr, a famous lingerie model, say, "Models are some of the most insecure people I've ever met."[2]

Counterfeit femininity says that real women are sexy, hot, free, edgy, and wild.

If sexual freedom is so beneficial, then why isn't it proving itself that way? Why are women still struggling with feelings of worthlessness?

We as Christian women need to take a step back. We need to look at the path sexual freedom takes us down. When we throw our arrows in the wrong direction, we end up with a jumble of feelings—negative ones. Insecurity. Worthlessness. Confusion about beauty. Confusion about sex. Confusion about femininity.

It's time to rethink sex. It's time to rethink beauty. It's time to reject counterfeit femininity and refocus our attention on the bull's-eye. You'll discover exactly what that looks like in the chapters to come.

Throw Away Your Mud Pies

We opened this chapter with the story of Katie Jones, a young woman who adopted the Three Pillars of Counterfeit Femininity:

liberation, independence, and sexual freedom. She believed her purpose and fulfillment could be found in the culture's definition of a successful woman, but she was wrong.

Our culture consistently pushes us, as women, to welcome a lifestyle built on these three qualities. Most of us have taken the bait at one time or another. We've acquiesced to different aspects of each idea. We've believed that somehow they can bring us the fulfillment and purpose we long for.

Personally, neither of us liked the results that counterfeit femininity produced in our lives. It never satisfied us or delivered what it had promised. Women all across the world are experiencing the same thing. They've built their lives on the foundation of counterfeit femininity and are unhappy with the results.

A study called *The Paradox of Declining Female Happiness* discovered a shocking reality: "By many objective measures the lives of women in the United States have improved over the past 35 years, yet . . . measures of subjective well-being indicate that women's happiness has declined both absolutely and relative to men."[3]

Another popular website for women agrees with the above quote. The author said, "We honestly believed that if we worked hard, we could have it all and more. Yet so many of us have ended up lonely, exhausted and broken-hearted, with far less of what we bargained for."[4]

Instead of floating in the current and following the popular trends for womanhood, let's jump onto the shore and rethink this thing. In what ways have you bought into the three pillars? Do you believe liberating yourself from God's design will give you a satisfying purpose?

For us, the answer is no. We have never found long-term satisfaction by embracing counterfeit femininity.

It's time for something better.

According to C. S. Lewis, "We are half-hearted creatures, fooling about with drink and sex and ambition when infinite joy is offered

We have never found long-term satisfaction by embracing counterfeit femininity.

us, like an ignorant child who wants to go on making mud pies in a slum because he cannot imagine what is meant by the offer of a holiday at the sea. We are far too easily pleased."[5]

Women, we were created for more than mud pies. We need to throw them away and chase after something more satisfying. Something that has proven to be successful. God has so much more in store for you as a woman. He has a tried-and-true plan and a godly purpose that is a billion times better than counterfeit femininity.

CHAPTER 3

STUDY GUIDE

Hitting God's bull's-eye for womanhood leads to satisfaction, while everything else leads to endless pursuits.

1. Who are the Katie Joneses in your life? In what ways do you compare yourself to them?

   _____

   _____

   _____

2. When you see women's magazines displayed in a store, what thoughts run through your mind? Write down four ways magazine images have affected your view of womanhood.

   _____

   _____

   _____

   _____

3. The two of us shared our stories of how we bought into the lies of counterfeit femininity. Now it's time for you to do some soul-searching. Write down a short description of how you are currently being influenced by the three pillars:

LIBERATION:_____

_____

_____

INDEPENDENCE:_____

_____

_____

SEXUAL FREEDOM: _____

_____

_____

4. Have you been satisfied with the results of counterfeit femininity in your life? Why or why not?

_____

_____

_____

MAKE IT HAPPEN *Today*

Do you own any magazines, movies, books, etc. that encourage counterfeit femininity? If so, we challenge you to trash one of those items today (feel free to get rid of more though!).

Part 2

GETTING BACK TO GOD'S DESIGN

4. GOOD-BYE MODELING, HELLO NEW DIRECTION

Bethany and I were both in our early twenties and desperately curious. The seed that had taken root in our hearts as young girls was finally coming to bloom. We wanted to explore the modeling world. Truthfully, our hopes weren't that high. We assumed, outside of a miracle, that our moral convictions and living as models probably wouldn't jive. We didn't want to miss an opportunity based on assumptions though. We wanted to know for sure. We had to see firsthand.

We sat in our living room with our parents and discussed the details. They explained the potential pitfalls and tried to convince us to let go of the idea and move on. But we weren't budging. With their grudging approval, we contacted our modeling recruiters.

Kristen's Modeling Journey

Several days after my nerve-wracking interview with Jessica Brown, which I shared earlier, I got a call saying the agency wanted me to join the team! According to Jessica, it seemed my personal convictions and the modeling world could go hand in hand. The agency prided itself on being "family friendly" and "anti-nudity." I was absolutely thrilled. I immediately went back to Jessica's office to sign a one-year contract. To top things off, I also signed a written agreement saying I would never be forced to do a job or wear something I wasn't comfortable with. Score! This was looking like a dream come true.

I started working for the agency part-time with a modeling job here and there. Things seemed to be going pretty well—until about halfway through the year. Jessica began sending me jobs that crossed the line of my personal boundaries. She would say things like, "You'll never become something big unless you take every job you can get."

As time went on, the pressure increased. I could sense that unless I was going to compromise my standards, I would not be welcomed long term. I started to dread the phone calls and emails. I knew I was being pressured, and I didn't like it.

After several more months of awkward interactions with people at the agency, I was ready to face the hard truth. I knew they weren't interested in having me on as a "dead weight." They wanted to make their agency's name known, and they needed their models to help them accomplish that.

Success in the modeling industry is based on how high one can climb the modeling ladder. I was no longer interested in climbing any higher. I imagined myself five to ten years down the road and didn't like what I saw. I knew I would have to compromise. I knew that every time I lowered the bar, I would feel pressure to lower it again. I knew that I would become completely obsessed with my outward appearance. I knew drugs, alcohol, and eating disorders were rampant in the modeling world. I knew I would eventually have to move, and by default, the other models would become my family. My romantic dreams of modeling were coming head-to-head with reality.

My romantic dreams of modeling were coming head-to-head with reality.

I decided to make a list of pros and cons to help myself honestly evaluate the situation. My list of pros contained two things: (1) I could make pretty good money, and (2) I could have the title *model.* My list of cons went on and on. Too many to list.

The answer was clear. I chose to quit after my one-year contract ended and instead focus my attention in a new direction.

Bethany's Modeling Journey

My (Bethany's) modeling journey was the polar opposite of Kristen's. Without realizing it, I chose an agency that missed the "family friendly and anti-nudity" memo. Remember Jeff?

Let's just say he wasn't the type of guy who concerned himself with other people's comforts. He wasn't interested in wasting his time. During the interview, he must have sensed my hesitation.

Jeff decided to nip my hesitation in the bud and make himself very clear. He said, "I'm not looking for the most beautiful girls to work in my company. I would rather take a less attractive girl who is willing to do more. I want my models to make it to the top. In order to do that, you have to take whatever jobs you can get."

I didn't know what to say. I was not interested in showing off my body to the world. I wasn't desperate for this job. I was just exploring the opportunity. Jeff interrupted my thoughts and continued his rant, "Do you realize that over this past weekend, we had an entire casting call? This entire building was filled with girls dying for a chance to model with our company. Our agency typically never conducts private interviews outside of the casting calls. This is a special exception, young lady."

At this point in the interview, I had heard enough. I thought, *Run for your life, Bethany*, but on the outside I just smiled and nodded, waiting for him to finish. I could not wait to leave Jeff's office. I was completely grossed out and disturbed. The nearly nude pictures covering the walls. The way he described the "catwalk."

Him clarifying that he only wanted models "willing to show all." The way he talked about women. Gross. Gross. Gross.

Jeff and I went through a few more formalities before we acknowledged that this job was not for me. Before I left Jeff's office, he gave me one final piece of advice: "When you get out from under your parents' roof and gain some independence, try becoming comfortable in your own skin. Then come back, and we can talk some more." By "becoming comfortable in [my] own skin," he meant willing to strip down for the camera. *Okay . . . um. Thanks for the advice—not.*

I left that day absolutely sure that I never wanted to be a model.

I shook his hand, walked out of the agency, got in my car, and immediately doused my hands with hand sanitizer. I left that day absolutely sure that I never wanted to be a model. I didn't want to work for guys like Jeff. I didn't want to sell my image. I didn't want to compete with thousands of other women. I didn't want to take off all my clothes. I wasn't willing to trade in my life for the title *model*. I was through with that dream, and I wasn't looking back.

Putting Our Modeling Dreams to Rest

Through those short-lived modeling experiences, our wishes came true. We no longer had to assume. We'd seen firsthand. One sneak peek into the industry was enough. Everything about the lifestyle of a model was unappealing to us. The constant pressure to look amazing. The daily competition to beat out other models. The stress of always trying to look better. Be skinnier. Have clearer skin. Get rid of cellulite, wrinkles, and pimples. Not to mention the eating disorders, drugs, alcohol, and creepy photographers.

The idea of modeling sounded romantic until it became a possible reality. The facts were icky, and we wanted nothing to do with it.

With our dreams of modeling finally put to rest, it was time to seriously consider God's purpose and plan for our lives. We knew God had more in store for us. We knew God created us as females on purpose and for a purpose. We understood the basics of our gender and femininity, but we wanted to go deeper. We wanted to understand God's bull's-eye for us as women. This was our one shot at life. We wouldn't get a redo. This was it. We didn't want to waste it. We didn't want to spend our lives aiming at the wrong target.

The idea of modeling sounded romantic until it became a possible reality.

Moving in a Better Direction

Imagine yourself standing at a trailhead with multiple trail options. You look carefully down each one. You study the map. You watch as other people choose their path and start hiking. You look at the map and realize that whichever path you choose is the path you will hike for several hours. What if you don't like the path? What if you get halfway through and realize you picked a bad one? You look at your map one more time and decide to go for it. Fingers crossed, you hope you made the best decision.

That's exactly how both of us felt after the modeling experience. We felt like we were at the trailhead of life. There were various paths to choose from, but which one was the best to go down? Whichever path each of us chose would determine the course of the next several years of our lives—if not our entire lives.

We didn't want to get halfway down the trail and realize, *Oh no! We should have picked a different path*. We weren't interested in backtracking. We didn't want to waste our energy. We didn't want to waste our time working toward the wrong end goal. We wanted to start right. We wanted to study the map carefully and make sure we were heading in the best direction.

At this point in our lives, we definitely had a better-than-average understanding of our femininity. We were very blessed to have parents who loved each other and took the time to train and mentor us as young girls. They gave us a strong foundation to work from and pointed us in the right direction. Having that groundwork was huge. However, we eventually had to make our lives our own. We couldn't do everything according to "what Mommy and Daddy said." Our beliefs had to guide us. We had to own our choices.

We didn't want to waste our time working toward the wrong end goal.

Oddly enough, we had never taken the time to seriously pray over our future. Yeah, we had prayed over certain aspects of our future like, "God, should I accept this basketball scholarship?" "God, should I attend Bible school?" "God, should I enter into a relationship with that young man?" We prayed over the specifics for our lives, but neither of us had ever sat down and asked, "God, how can I best serve and glorify you?"

Thankfully, God got a hold of us before we plunged down a specific path. He used our modeling interviews and experiences to encourage us to look ahead and seriously consider where we were going.

We started asking questions that would eventually direct us to the path we are now on. We each asked, "God, how do you want me to use my femininity for your glory? What do you have to say about motherhood, marriage, purity, work, and romance?" We each wondered, *If I continue going down the path I'm on, where will I end up? Where will this path take me in five years? In ten years? Is that where I want to be? Is that God's best?*

Determined to find answers, we bought dozens of Christian books on womanhood. Every topic. Every style of writing. Everything. We studied hard. We attended Christian conferences and women's Bible studies. We took this extremely seriously. Our futures were at stake as we fought to figure out God's purpose for our lives as women.

With months of studying under our belt, the path of God-defined femininity came more clearly into view. We started to own our beliefs, letting them shape and become a part of us. And they began to influence our thinking and determine our choices.

Once we understood God's design and purpose for us as females, his bull's-eye

Once we understood God's design and purpose for us as females, his bull's-eye became clear.

became clear. We no longer felt confused or worried about the future. We were no longer aiming our arrows in whichever way culture was pointing. We could clearly see the difference between counterfeit femininity and God-defined femininity. We finally had a clear vision of how God wanted us, as women, to use our lives for his glory. In the next chapter, we'll explore exactly what that looks like.

CHAPTER 4
STUDY GUIDE

STASH IT IN YOUR HEART

Choosing to live a God-defined lifestyle is one of the best decisions you will ever make.

1. Have you ever stopped to think about the path your life is on? If you stay on your current path, where will you end up five years down the road?

   _____

   _____

   _____

2. We challenge you to take some time over the next seven days to pray about your current path, as well as your future plans.

   Dear God, please open my eyes to areas of my life in which I am not honoring you. Help me discern, through your Word, whether my life plans align with your heart for my womanhood. Help me not to waste time and energy pursuing a dead-end path. Examine my heart and adjust my desires to align with your truth. Please help me gain a God-defined vision for my womanhood and my future. Amen.

3. After much prayer, we each realized God had given us a passion for ministering to women. What passions and gifts has God given to you?

_____

_____

_____

4. How can you use those passions and gifts to serve God?

_____

_____

_____

MAKE IT HAPPEN *Today*

As Proverbs 29:18 says, "Where there is no vision, the people perish." In two or three sentences, write down what you think this verse means.

_____

_____

_____

5. GENDER, YOU ARE OH SO MAGNIFICENT

Imagine walking into a clothing store and the sales clerk approaches you and says, "Welcome to our store, sir . . . or ma'am."

Shocked, you raise your eyebrows and say, "Um . . . I'm a *ma'am*, not a *sir*."

"Oh, pardon me!" he says apologetically. "I just didn't want to assume. Better safe than sorry these days."

Offended and confused, you walk away wondering why someone would ever refer to you as a sir.

It's unlikely that would actually happen to you today, but it might become a reality at some point in the future. In fact, it's already happening at a preschool in Sweden.

The taxpayer-funded preschool Egalia has decided that gender-specific language and actions are damaging to children and society. Instead of referring to children as "boys" and "girls" or using pronouns such as "him" and "her," staff members refer to everyone as "friends."

An article from *The Star* further points out, "From the colour and placement of toys to the choice of books, every detail has been carefully planned to make sure the children don't fall into gender stereotypes. Nearly all the children's books deal with homosexual couples, single parents or adopted children. There are no 'Snow White,' 'Cinderella' or other classic fairy tales seen as cementing stereotypes."

Director Lotta Rajalin says staff members also try to help the children discover new ideas when they play.

"A concrete example could be when they're playing 'house' and the role of the mom already is taken and they start to squabble," she says. "Then we suggest two moms or three moms and so on."[1]

The underlying goal of this Swedish preschool is to erase all gender distinctions between males and females. It's striving to create a world in which gender doesn't exist and each person can "choose" what kind of person they want to be.

Although many people still consider this kind of thinking extreme, it's slowly gaining mainstream popularity. From gender-neutral clothing stores to gender-neutral bathrooms to gender-neutral baby names to gender-neutral toys, society is subtly promoting the idea that gender doesn't matter. Female? Male? Who cares? We're all the same. We should all do the same things.

Instead of promoting our beautiful and unique design as women, we're told it's really not that special. We're really no different from men. And that mind-set offends the two of us. As women, we're proud of who God made us to be and don't appreciate being forced into a neutral mold. We don't have to be the "same" as men to have value and equality. We know God designed females and males to be equally valuable in worth but purposely different in roles.

Sadly, though, many Christian churches and communities are accepting this gender-neutral messaging. Instead of fighting for our unique differences, we're buying into the lie that sameness is better. We're buying into the lies that say masculinity and femininity are interchangeable. That husbands and wives should share the same roles. That there's no difference between dads and moms. Our culture is attempting to erase all gender distinctions from our vocabulary, and many of us are taking the bait—hook, line, and sinker.

Maybe you haven't bought into the lies about gender. But our guess is you've probably unknowingly bought into a few gender lies (we have!). It's almost impossible not to. Our culture's modern view on gender permeates almost every TV show, movie, song, magazine, and book. It's everywhere. Like a wolf in sheep's clothing, this worldview is subtly eating the church and families alive.

Soaking Up the Message

The results of throwing out God-defined gender roles have been devastating to our society. Men don't know how to be men anymore. Women don't know how to be women anymore. Marriages are in shambles. Relationships are spiraling downward. Homes are more like hotels. Kitchens are more like drive-thrus. The family unit is being destroyed from the inside out.

Instead of turning to God's Word first and allowing him to inform our worldview on gender, many of us do the opposite. We call ourselves Christians. We go to church. We try to read our Bibles on a fairly regular basis. But when we get down to it, God's Word isn't the deciding factor in what we believe. We read our Bibles and say, "That's a nice story. Hmmm, encouraging." Then we take notice of the world's messages, opening our ears to the many ideas and soaking up what they tell us. We allow the world to inform our beliefs about gender. We allow culture to tell us how to live as women.

Instead of turning to God's Word first and allowing him to inform our worldview on gender, many of us do the opposite.

God's Word becomes nothing more than an inspirational book of encouraging teachings. As a result, we, as Christian women, reap many of the same consequences we see in mainstream society. If we want better results for our womanhood and our families, we have to get back to God's design for gender.

Searching for the Truth

Even though the two of us grew up in a great Christian family, we had to establish our own personal convictions. Like we mentioned earlier, it wasn't until after our modeling experiences that we really started searching. And in our searching, we began to understand how radically different God's design for gender really is.

So what did we do? We explored God's Word—the Bible. After spending some time studying the book of Genesis, God's design for man and woman became apparent like never before. By studying Scripture, we laid aside the ideas of our culture and said, "God, show us your design. We humbly submit to your plan." Then, and only then, did God's Word take full authority in our lives. Then, and only then, did our hearts soften toward biblical womanhood. Once God's Word informed our worldview, we radically changed the way we lived.

> *Once God's Word informed our worldview, we radically changed the way we lived.*

If you want God's Word to transform your heart and your life, you must allow it to inform your worldview.

Jump back in time with us as we check out the most romantic love story of all time. The love story in which gender was born.

She Was His Girl

All eyes were on him. There was a shift in the wind. Something magnificent was about to take place. Dozens of newly created animals hovered near the tree line. They were watching. They were waiting. The dirt began to stir. A pile began to form. God reached his hands into the dust to form and shape it. He added a little more. He molded the ground into a mysterious shape. The animals locked their gaze on this motionless mass. Then something amazing happened. Something extraordinary. God bent down and breathed into the nostrils of this lifeless pile. The animals held their gaze. Then the unimaginable happened. The pile began to move. God took a step back to watch.

Breathing in and out, the pile began to rise. Slowly pushing off the ground, the creature stood to its feet. As the dust fell to the ground, the animals stared in amazement. What was this thing? It was unlike anything God had made before. God smiled at his newest creation. Unlike the animals, this creature smiled back. For the first time ever, a human being stood before God. "Then the LORD God formed the man of dust from the ground and breathed into his nostrils the breath of life, and the man became a living creature" (Gen. 2:7).

The first human had arrived, but he didn't have a place to live. God wasn't done with miracles yet. The Bible says, "And the LORD God planted a garden in Eden, in the east, and there he put the man whom he had formed. The LORD God took the man and put him in the garden of Eden to work it and keep it" (Gen. 2:8, 15). God planted a special garden, a home, for Adam to live and work in. As he explored this amazing land of paradise, God approached him. He needed to give Adam a few housekeeping rules. He lovingly looked at Adam with concern in his eyes and said, "You may surely eat of every tree of the garden, but of the tree of the knowledge of good and evil you shall not eat, for in the day that you eat of it you shall surely die" (Gen. 2:16–17). Adam nodded in understanding.

Every animal had a mate, but he had no one.

God walked away but returned shortly. This time with a trail of animals and birds behind him. Pointing to the animals, God explained that Adam was in charge of naming them. All of them. One by one the animals stood before Adam, and he gave them their names. As the last kangaroo bounced away, Adam noticed something for the first time. He was alone. He was the only human on earth. Every animal had a mate, but he had no one. As Adam stared longingly into the distance, God knew it was time. Adam took a few steps, then laid down on a soft grassy patch to rest. Little did he know what was about to happen.

After some time, his eyes slowly blinked open. The sun shimmered through the trees as a gentle breeze blew. The fresh air drew him out of his deep sleep. Rolling over in the velvety grass, he felt something strange. Something was different. Glancing to the right, he noticed some animals watching him. Stretching his arms and yawning, he looked in the other direction. He froze. A soft gasp escaped his mouth.

She was made for him, and she knew it. She loved it.

His eyes locked onto a mysterious creature standing before him. She was breathtaking. Adam's mouth dropped open as he realized what this incredible creature was. Feeling his side, it clicked. She was for him! He jumped to his feet and excitedly exclaimed, "This at last is bone of my bones and flesh of my flesh; she shall be called Woman, because she was taken out of Man" (Gen. 2:23).

Eve smiled as she watched Adam's excitement. She was made for him, and she knew it. She loved it. Adam walked over and gently took her hand. "Come on," he said joyfully. "There's so much to see in the garden. I'll teach you everything you need to know."

Hand in hand, with perfect love, she followed her new husband through paradise.

Once upon a Time, Marriage Was Perfect

Do you ever wonder what those first moments in the garden looked like? Do you ever wonder what Adam and Eve looked like? We wonder those things all the time! Were they tall, short, fair skinned, dark skinned? Would we consider him handsome and her beautiful? Were their teeth sparkly white? So many questions. Whatever they looked like, they were perfect. We do know that much. They were made from God's hands.

Before Adam and Eve were formed, God had a blank slate. There were no humans on the earth. He could have created anything he wanted. Anything. But what did he do? He created two distinct genders. One male and one female. As God formed the first humans, he was intentional about every move. He did things in a specific order for a specific reason. He could have simplified things by creating only one gender. But why would such a complex God want to do that? He's way too creative. Instead, he created some diversity. Some excitement. He made two distinct genders that complement each other.

The order in which God chose to create Adam and Eve is fascinating. It sheds a lot of light on gender roles. Most people glaze over the book of Genesis with a "been there, heard that" attitude. But if you stop to take a closer look, you might be fascinated too.

For starters, God created Adam before the Garden of Eden existed. It wasn't until after Adam was formed that God planted the garden and set Adam in it (Gen. 2:7–8). Adam was given rules, jobs, and responsibility long before Eve entered the scene (v. 15). Why? Because God was helping Adam become a leader. He was giving him some hands-on practice. God was preparing Adam for his role as a husband, father, and leader. He was in charge of cultivating the garden (vv. 15, 19–20). He was in charge of naming all the animals. He was in charge of understanding and obeying the garden rules (vv. 16–17). Adam was taking care of his new domain before Eve came onto the scene. These details are an extremely important part of the story. We can't glaze over them, because they inform us on God's design for gender.

When Adam was finally established in his position, God knew it was time. Adam was ready. "The Lord God said, 'It is not good that the man should be alone; I will make him a helper fit for him'" (v. 18). (We're going to dig into the true definition of that word helper in the next chapter.)

Adam and Eve's marriage was a perfect union full of blissful harmony.

Adam and Eve's marriage was a perfect union full of blissful harmony. Eve respected her husband unconditionally, and he cherished her unreservedly. Life was perfect. Literally. They never fought over whose role was more important. They knew they each had distinct, yet equally valuable, jobs. And life was wonderful.

So why are gender distinctions so important, and why does it matter to us today?

Equally Valuable but Purposely Different

I (Kristen) really enjoy dancing. Primarily swing dancing. Several years ago my husband, Zack, and I decided to take swing dancing lessons. Ouch. This was a hilarious learning experience for both of us. We stood there facing each other, my hands gently resting on top of his. The music started and we began to move. Step, step, rock step. Step, step, rock step. We looked pretty good. Until Zack attempted to spin me. Trying to anticipate his move, I completely messed everything up. I went one way and he went the other. The dance instructor noticed our blunder and quickly came to the rescue.

"Okaaaay," he said. "You have a common problem." Looking at me, he continued, "You cannot anticipate your husband's moves. You have to relax your body. Keep your arms stiff, keep your wrists firm and allow him to move you around."

"Oh. I didn't realize I was doing that," I said. "Got it. Thanks for the tip."

After that night, Zack and I decided that dancing is great practice for marriage. If we want to become great dancers, we need to understand some basic rules. Dancing requires a leader and a follower—two people who understand their part and do it. It requires teamwork and unanimity. If one person drops the ball, the dance doesn't work like it's supposed to. One role isn't more valuable than the other. They're equally important but different. Both people must contribute to have success.

Gender works the same way (you knew that was coming). God designed the male with a specific role and purpose to fulfill. Likewise, he designed the female with a specific role and purpose to fulfill. When the male and female function according to God's design, the dance works. When they don't, they experience blunders and confusion.

Just like dancing partners, one gender is not more valuable than the other. Both are equally valuable to God. In fact, when God created the human race, do you know what he said? "Let us make man in our image, after our likeness. So God created man in his own image, in the image of God he created him; male and female he created them" (Gen. 1:26, 27). Bam! Case closed. This verse clearly tells us that both genders are made in God's image. Both genders are equally valuable.

When the male and female function according to God's design, the dance works.

Males and females were created to reflect different parts of God's character and nature. And in doing so, we bring God immense glory. As the book *True Woman 101* points out, "Men were created to reflect the strength, love, and self-sacrifice of Christ. Women were created to reflect the responsiveness, grace, and beauty of the bride He redeemed."[2] As females, we glorify God the most when we embrace and live out his design for our gender.

Have you ever stopped to think about the unique features God gave to us as women? Seriously! Our bodies are built differently than a man's. We typically have softer skin, smaller muscles, and slighter frames. We have the capacity to get pregnant and carry a baby inside of our wombs. We tend to be more relational and nurturing.

As females, we glorify God the most when we embrace and live out his design for our gender.

God hardwired us to be different from men for a reason. And that reason should matter to us. The book of Genesis proves that the school in Sweden has it all wrong. God created us to be females on purpose. Our unique features and gifts should inform us on God's design for us. We'll explore more about our unique design in the next chapter.

Caution: You Are Now Entering the Battle of the Sexes

When God created Adam and Eve, their lives were perfect. They were completely unaffected by sin. It was easy for Eve to fulfill her role as Adam's wife. She accepted God's design for her femininity. She delighted in it. It was easy for Adam to lead selflessly. It came naturally to him.

Then one day a slimy snake slithered onto the scene and strategically targeted Eve. All it took was one little question. One little seed of doubt. "Did God actually say, 'You shall not eat of any tree in the garden?'" (Gen. 3:1).

Notice what Satan did here. He deliberately questioned God's authority. "Did God actually say . . . ?" Satan knows that God's Word is the foundation for all truth. If he can get us to question what God says, then he can deceive us into believing a lie. And that's exactly what he did to Eve. She questioned God and her foundation crumbled. She took a bite of the forbidden fruit and then gave some to Adam.

What was the consequence of their disobedience? Sin. The trust, love, peace, and security they enjoyed were shattered. Their lives were instantly infested with sin. Their punishments were sex-specific, making it harder for them to function according to God's design. Sin messed up Eve's womanhood. Sin messed up Adam's manhood. At that moment, the battle of the sexes was born. Perfect harmony was gone forever.

Fast forward to today, and we're still reaping the consequences of Adam and Eve's sin. It's the reason we push against God-defined gender roles. It's why gender has become so convoluted. It's what causes us, as Christian women, to struggle to embrace God's design. Instead of men and women living together in perfect harmony, we're now pitted against one another.

Sin messed up Eve's womanhood. Sin messed up Adam's manhood.

Satan is still alive and well today. "Be sober-minded; be watchful. Your adversary the devil prowls around like a roaring lion, seeking someone to devour" (1 Pet. 5:8). He slithers around whispering the same question in our ears that he did to Eve. "*Did God actually say* men and women are different?" "*Did God actually say* femininity matters?" "*Did God actually say* gender roles are important?" "*Did God actually say* motherhood is valuable?" "*Did God actually say* womanhood is unique?" Satan uses the same tactics he used on Eve. His goal is to have all of us question the authority of God's Word.

He knows if we question the Bible, we will open our ears to other opinions. He knows we will look somewhere else for answers.

While the damage of sin has been great, thankfully, the story isn't over. All hope is not lost.

Girl, Your Gender Is Worth Fighting For

Our womanhood has been scarred but not severed. Damaged but not broken. We serve a God who is in the restoration business.

What Satan meant for evil, God will use for good. And it starts with you. It starts with us.

Despite what society thinks, the gender-neutral movement will not lead to restoration. It will not lead to fulfillment. It can't. Why? Because its foundation is built on a lie—a lie that says lasting happiness and fulfillment can come outside of God's design. It's the same lie Eve believed. In the end, this movement will leave women (and men) feeling empty, hopeless, and alone.

The only sure way to restore our womanhood is to get back to God's design for gender. We have to believe what God's Word says and build our lives on his truth. Every Christian woman has to make a crucial choice. A choice to follow God's Word instead of listening to the world. A choice to take a step of faith and embrace biblical gender roles.

This isn't an easy task though. It's going to take strong women. Women who love the Lord. Women who want to fight for truth. Women who are willing to swim against the current.

> *The only sure way to restore our womanhood is to get back to God's design for gender.*

CHAPTER 5
STUDY GUIDE

*As females, we glorify God
the most when we embrace and live out
his design for our gender.*

1. How has the gender-neutral mind-set influenced your thinking?

   _____

   _____

   _____

2. Who or what is influencing your worldview about gender?

   On a scale of 1–10 (1 being no influence and 10 being a lot of influence), how much are each of the following areas influencing you?

TV Shows	1	2	3	4	5	6	7	8	9	10
Music	1	2	3	4	5	6	7	8	9	10
Secular Books	1	2	3	4	5	6	7	8	9	10
Christian Books	1	2	3	4	5	6	7	8	9	10
Movies	1	2	3	4	5	6	7	8	9	10
School	1	2	3	4	5	6	7	8	9	10
Work/Co-workers	1	2	3	4	5	6	7	8	9	10
Friends	1	2	3	4	5	6	7	8	9	10
Family Members	1	2	3	4	5	6	7	8	9	10
Church	1	2	3	4	5	6	7	8	9	10

| Social Media | 1 2 3 4 5 6 7 8 9 10 |
| The Bible | 1 2 3 4 5 6 7 8 9 10 |

According to your answers, which areas are influencing you the most?

_____

_____

_____

3. What do you think? Circle your answer.

True or False: It's okay for me to change my gender if I want to.

True or False: The female gender is less valuable than the male gender.

True or False: The book of Genesis is outdated and no longer applies.

True or False: God created Adam and Eve at the exact same time.

True or False: I can find lasting fulfillment outside of God's design for gender.

If you circled False on all the questions, you are spot on. If not, take some time to study God's Word and make sure his truth is informing your beliefs.

4. Read Genesis 2. In your own words, what does the Bible reveal to you about God's design for gender?

_____

_____

_____

MAKE IT HAPPEN *Today*

Take some time to humbly bow before your Creator and pray the following:

God, show me your design for my gender. Open my eyes to areas of my life in which I am resisting your design. I confess that I struggle to obey your Word. Help me humbly submit to your plan for my life. May I glorify you with my womanhood and humbly reflect your image. Amen.

6. MODERN CHIC, MEET BIBLICAL WOMANHOOD

We (Kristen and Bethany, along with two of our siblings, Timothy and Rebekah) pulled through the guarded gate and headed to the guest parking lot. After we got out of the car, our camera crew (Timothy and Rebekah) rummaged through the trunk and pulled out supplies. They tested the cameras and said, "Ready when you are."

Heading into the heart of a local university campus to interview strangers wasn't necessarily our idea of a fun afternoon. So why were we doing it? The two of us wanted to find out what the average person thought about gender design. More specifically, we wanted to know what they thought the purpose of being a girl was.

We found a spot busy with people, set up the cameras, and waited to stop people for a surprise interview.

"Hey! We are doing video interviews for an upcoming project," we explained to the first woman we approached. "You look like the perfect girl to ask some questions."

"Me? Uh, okay. What's the topic?"

Phew! We got our first interview recorded.

Throughout the day we interviewed dozens of people. Girls. Guys. Couples. Groups of friends. All sorts. Every person was asked the same question first: "Besides physically, do you think there is a difference between guys and girls?" Without hesitation people answered "yes" and "yeah, I think so." Next we asked them, "What do you think the specific purpose of being a girl is? You know, distinctly from a guy?" That question was met with confused looks and complete speechlessness. One girl said, "Um . . . um, a purpose?" Another said, "I'm not sure. I don't know."

We found a spot busy with people, set up the cameras, and waited to stop people for a surprise interview.

After filming for what seemed like an eternity, Timothy looked through the footage and said, "That's a wrap!"

Later in the week as the two of us looked through the footage, we realized a recurring theme. Every person we interviewed agreed that besides their physical characteristics, guys and girls are different. When we took it a step further and asked what they thought was the specific purpose of being a girl, they had no idea. Most of the interviewees were speechless. They couldn't verbalize even a hint of a clue.

The young people at the university are definitely not alone. We decided to take our questions to Christian circles and specifically ask the women what they thought. After talking to multiple Christian women, we realized that most of them have only a basic understanding of God's design for femininity. When asked the question, "What is the specific purpose of being a girl?," most typically responded hesitantly and with little confidence. Up until a few years ago, that's exactly how the two of us would have responded too. We had the basic idea but weren't sure how to practically live that out.

Gaining Confidence

Remember how we told you in chapter 5 about how we studied Scripture to gain a better understanding of God's design? Well, that's how we learned to confidently answer the questions above. With proper understanding, we no longer felt hesitant or shy about our purpose as females. We understood God's truths and were excited to live them out.

If you don't feel confident answering the question, What is the distinct purpose of being a woman?, we want to help you with that. Our hope is that by the end of this chapter you can feel completely sure of your womanhood and know God's specific design for you as a female.

Three Pillars of Biblical Womanhood

I (Bethany) was recently walking through an adorable gift shop in Estes Park, Colorado, with Kristen and her sister-in-law, Jacqueline. Like any good tourist, I was hoping to find one last souvenir. As I scanned the shelves, my eyes caught the title of a book that stopped me dead in my tracks. The title? *Everything Men Know about Women.* I first looked around to see if anyone was watching and then picked it up to read the back cover. What girl doesn't want to know what men are thinking about women? I know I do.

I took a deep breath, put my hands on both sides of the book, and mentally geared up for what I was about to read. And then I opened it. To my utter shock, the book was *blank.* I flipped through the pages front to back and back to front. No intro. No table of contents. Then it hit me. This was a joke book! It's often said women are so complex that men can't figure them out. I burst into laughter and ran to show Kristen. I played it up and said, "You won't believe it. Check out this book!" As soon as she opened it, she started laughing.

Thankfully, we aren't left with a blank book to figure out the purpose for our womanhood. The Bible offers us wisdom and principles we can apply to our lives.

Thankfully, we aren't left with a blank book to figure out the purpose for our womanhood.

The two of us want to take you through three biblical truths about femininity. We like to call these truths the Three Pillars of Biblical Womanhood.

Whether or not we realize it, our lives are built on either good or bad pillars. Chapter 3 introduced you to the bad pillars of counterfeit femininity. Those are things we do not want to build our lives on. In contrast, this chapter will show you three good pillars—the pillars of biblical womanhood.

Before you explore the first pillar, take a moment to pause and pray:

Dear God,

Thank you so much for showing me the ultimate example of love and sacrifice. Thank you for clearly laying out the basic principles of womanhood in the Bible. I pray that as I study the Three Pillars of Biblical Womanhood, you would soften my heart and remove any traces of pride. Please help me embrace your truth. Please help me desire your glory above all else in my life. I love you and long to honor you with all I am.

In Jesus's name, amen.

PILLAR #1: SHE HELPS OTHERS

Helper. When you read that word, what comes to mind? Do you think of a successful woman or a woman being treated like a doormat? Helper. Does it ignite in you a desire to jump into a helper role? Some of us might wish God would take a whiteout pen and remove the word *helper* from the Bible.

But why is that? Why do we shriek at the word? Why do we despise this aspect of our feminine design? We (Bethany and Kristen) like to describe this problem as an underappreciation for God's design of the helper. It's not a very fancy description, but it's all we could come up with. When we, as women, don't have a solid understanding of God's definition for the word *helper*, we end up rolling our eyes at it. We believe you can gain a new appreciation (yes, even an excitement) for this word if you look at its original meaning.

The first pillar of biblical womanhood is titled "She Helps Others." In the last chapter, we discussed the importance of gender and the beauty of accepting our unique design as females. Remember how we recounted when Adam spotted Eve for the first time? Let's rewind to see what happened right before that moment.

Up until this point, God had said everything in creation was "good, good, good," and then we heard him say, "It is not good." For the first time in history, God said something wasn't good. Something was missing. God then pointed out the problem: "It is not good that the man should be alone" (Gen. 2:18a).

Adam probably cheered and said, "God, you're right! It is not good for me to be alone. I need someone. Please give me someone."

God had a solution in mind. "I will make him a helper fit for him" (Gen. 2:18b). Eve, a female, a helper, was God's solution to the problem.

Too often when we hear that tidbit of the creation account, we rush past it in hopes of ignoring it. We think, *Not the helper word. Run for your life!* Let's not make that mistake this time. Let's take a long pause and explore the true meaning of the word *helper*. We will never truly appreciate or fully embrace our design as helpers

> *We will never truly appreciate or fully embrace our design as helpers until we understand the original definition.*

until we understand the original definition of the word. So now it's time for a quick theology session.

> Two Hebrew terms in this verse [Genesis 2:18] provide important information to better understand the creation of Eve as the first woman. The word translated "helper" is the Hebrew term *'ezer*. This word is even used of God, sometimes, noting that He is our Helper (Ps. 115:9–11). We would certainly not view God, as a Helper, as subservient to humans, nor should we understand the role of "helper" in Genesis 2:18 as a position of subservience. The concept of an "ideal partner" seems to convey the thought best.
>
> The second important Hebrew word in this verse, translated "fit" is *kenegdo*. It literally means "according to the opposite of him." In other words, the focus is on an appropriate match. Eve was not created above or below Adam; she was complementary. The animals Adam had named each had an appropriate companion (Gen. 2:20), and Adam was given a fitting companion as well. Eve was "just right" for him.[1]

I (Kristen) love how God uses the exact same Hebrew word for helper to describe himself. God is perfect and holy. He would never use a word to describe himself that wasn't worthy. As women, we can take comfort in knowing we were designed after our perfect God.

Both single and married women are designed to help others.

Check out how short and sweet the dictionary defines the word *helper*: "Someone who helps another person with a job or task."[2] Ladies, that's our title in a nutshell. We are designed to find purpose in not only helping our husbands (or future husbands) but also helping people in general. Both single and married women are designed to help others.

Nancy DeMoss Wolgemuth and Mary Kassian will take us a step deeper in our study. They say:

Some people react negatively to the idea that woman was created to be a man's helper. They assume that this relegates her to a secondary role, where the woman is the servant and the man is the one who gets served: she is the one who unilaterally helps him. She "helps" him by picking up his dirty clothes and cooking his meals, for example. While a woman can help her husband domestically, this view of the role of helper misses the essential point.

Contrary to what some have suggested, "helper" is not a demeaning term that indicates a lesser status, or the type of help that assists in a trivial way. The Hebrew word (ezer) [like we just learned] is a powerful one. It's most often used with reference to the Lord being our helper (Ps. 33:20; 72:12). An "ezer" provides help that is absolutely and utterly indispensable.[3]

That is exactly what God had in mind when he created Eve. He was creating her to be "absolutely and utterly indispensable." He was creating her as Adam's opposite. He was creating her to help Adam bring glory to God. Ultimately, Adam's role as the leader and Eve's role as the helper have the same underlying purpose. It's all about serving and pointing others to Christ. Neither role is about us. They are both always about God. When serving God is our goal, having the title "helper" won't bother us. We can gratefully accept our God-defined position to bring honor to him.

Helping others is foundational in God's design for womanhood.

Where is your heart in all of this? Do you want to fully accept the title helper? Do you want to bring God glory by helping others succeed?

Remember, God used the word *helper* for himself (Ps. 115:9–11). Helping is noble and if done with a heart of humility, can be a beautiful reflection of Christ.

In a nutshell, here is your key takeaway for pillar #1: Helping others is foundational in God's design for womanhood.

PILLAR #2: SHE PRODUCES LIFE

In the heart of downtown Chicago, there is a massive museum that displays everything from a full-size submarine to baby chicks hatching in an incubator. One of my (Kristen's) favorite displays is on babies and pregnancy. I stood in awe as I walked through the "life display," which shows babies only weeks after conception up to nine month olds. Looking at the development and intricacy of God's design was literally breathtaking.

A real live baby grows inside a woman's womb for nine months, and then her body (usually) perfectly times itself to give birth when the baby is fully developed and ready to come out. It's nothing short of mind-blowing and miraculous. What's even more amazing is that out of the approximately seven billion people in the world, only half of those are even capable of doing what I just described.

Women. We are God's chosen gender to carry, develop, and birth new life (Gen. 3:20). The second pillar of biblical femininity is titled "She Produces Life." *She* is the key word in that sentence. *She* is the one who was made for this job. Pregnancy and birth are unique to the female gender alone. Never will a male be able to naturally experience this process. His body simply was not designed for this purpose. Obviously, a male is a key factor in impregnating a female, but after that the baby grows in and emerges from the woman's body.

We are God's chosen gender to carry, develop, and birth new life.

Producing life (both physically and spiritually) is at the core of womanhood. We, as women, were designed for this function.

As a result of the fall, not every woman is physically capable of carrying and birthing a child. And those women who are able to bear children will experience intense physical pain during the process. But even with these hardships and trials, women still have hope.

The physical aspects of our design are only an outward symbol of an inward reality. God's original design for the female body was intended to point to something much deeper than just birthing children. God was cluing us in on our makeup as women.

It doesn't matter if you are single, married with children, married without children, or past childbearing age, the truth about your life-producing design can be fulfilled in every season of life.

I (Bethany) love how Elisabeth Elliot, my spiritual hero in the faith, describes this truth. She says,

> Yours is the body of a woman. What does it signify? Is there invisible meaning in its visible signs—the softness, the smoothness, the lighter bones and muscle structure, the breasts, the womb? Are they utterly unrelated to what you yourself are? Isn't your identity intimately bound up with these material forms?[4]

God created us, as women, to be life givers. He created us with the ability to produce both physical and spiritual children.

Psalm 113:9 says, "He gives the childless woman a household, making her the joyful mother of children. Hallelujah!" (HCSB). God gives the childless woman "spiritual children" through the lives she impacts.

> God gives us different gifts and callings. The gift of marriage is not given to every woman, nor is the gift of bearing children. It is not a given that every woman will marry, or that married women will be able to bear children. What IS a given is that *all* women are called to be spiritually fruitful. The Lord wants all women—including single and childless women and women past childbearing age—to have a "household" and be the "joyful mother of children."[5]

When we, as women, choose to produce life (spiritual or physical), we imitate our Savior Jesus Christ. He chose to give up his life, so we as sinners could have eternal life. In the same way, when we give our time, service, and mentorship, we produce life as well.

No matter your season of life, you can live out this aspect of your design. You can be a life giver, which involves the spiritual condition of your heart and your mind-set more than anything. It means looking at God's physical design of your body and asking why he created you that way. It's your heart that says, "I am willing to produce life in the most helpful and appropriate way for this season of my life." As a single girl without kids, I (Bethany) will show you how I live this out in the next chapter.

Producing life is foundational in God's design for womanhood.

When you read "She Produces Life," what comes to mind? Do you think of your design as a female? Do you think of physical children? Do you think of spiritual children? Your life as a woman is so much more than just your physical makeup. Your physical body should always remind you of God's bigger goal for your womanhood. That is, being a life producer.

In a nutshell, here is your key takeaway for pillar #2: Producing life is foundational in God's design for womanhood.

PILLAR #3: SHE NURTURES RELATIONSHIPS

Recently our mom told us she was meeting up with a friend at a coffee shop. Typically, when either of us thinks of a coffee date with one of our girlfriends, we imagine a good two- to three-hour talk. Not our mom. Her coffee dates typically last from six to eight hours. She knows how to communicate like a pro. She asks great questions, listens intently, and shares deeply from her heart. She is a beautiful example of a godly woman who knows how to nurture relationships.

So far we've discussed the first two pillars of biblical womanhood. We've seen the importance of our role as a helper. We've dug deep into the meaning of being a life producer. It's time to explore the third and final pillar of biblical womanhood. Pillar #3 is titled "She Nurtures Relationships."

In the first pillar, we talked through Genesis 2:18 and focused on the word *helper*. Let's look at that same passage and talk about a different but extremely important word.

"Then the LORD God said, 'It is not good that the man should be alone; I will make him a helper fit for him'" (Gen. 2:18). God said a helper fit *for* him. God reemphasized this key word a few verses later by stating, "But *for* Adam there was not found a helper fit *for* him" (Gen. 2:20, emphasis added). God seems to be making a very clear point. Eve was created *for* someone.

The two of us find the word *for* intriguing because it points to a specific area of our design as women. According to Nancy DeMoss Wolgemuth and Mary Kassian,

> Being created "for someone" indicates that God created the female to be a highly relational creature. In contrast to the male, her identity isn't based on work nearly as much as on how well she connects and relates to others. *Forming deep relational bonds is at the core of what it means to be a woman.*[6]

God chose to create women to be highly relational beings. The fact that we were created for someone helps us understand our inner desire to connect in a deep and meaningful way. It's part of who we are. It's hardwired inside of us. We can't change that aspect of our womanhood. We were created to find satisfaction in deep, meaningful, God-honoring relationships.

God chose to create women to be highly relational beings.

Just look around, and you'll quickly see the results of this relational bent. Have you ever noticed how women often travel in packs (or at least in pairs) to restrooms? Why is that? Because we like being together, no matter where we are. It's such a female thing. Can you image men doing that? Never.

According to recent studies, it's estimated that women speak an average of 20,000 words a day, while men speak an average of only 7,000 words.[7] We, as women, like to talk and connect with other human beings.

Many women (like our mom) can get together for breakfast, lunch, dinner, and coffee to chat for hours on end. Women can meet for the first time, and before you know it they are pulling out tissues and crying together. Why? Because women, in general, love connecting relationally.

The bottom line is this: women are relational beings because God designed us to be that way. He wants us first to fill ourselves with him so that we then go out and share God's love with others. Like we've said before, it doesn't matter how young or old you are, or whether you're married or single, every woman in every stage of life has the ability to nurture relationships for God's glory.

You can nurture relationships wherever God has you right now. You can nurture a relationship with your parent(s). You can nurture a relationship with your sibling(s). You can nurture a relationship with your husband. You can nurture a relationship with your child(ren). You can nurture a relationship with your neighbor(s). You may never know the impact you've had on someone because of your decision to nurture a relationship with them.

Nurturing relationships is foundational in God's design for womanhood.

Where is your heart in regard to this third and final pillar of biblical femininity?

The eighteenth-century American poet William Ross Wallace wrote a famous poem titled "The Hand That Rocks the Cradle Is the Hand That Rules the World." Never underestimate the indispensable role of nurturing relationships.

Imagine the impact you could have on a young person's life by choosing to selflessly nurture a relationship with them.

In a nutshell, here is your key takeaway for pillar #3: Nurturing relationships is foundational in God's design for womanhood.

True Success Defined by God

The Three Pillars of Biblical Womanhood are God's bull's-eye of true success. Helping others, producing life, and nurturing relationships are the qualities each of us, as women, posseses. When you pick up your arrow and aim it at the bull's-eye of biblical femininity, you acknowledge that God's ways truly are best. Lasting fulfillment and authentic worth are found only when you build your life on God's design for womanhood.

CHAPTER 6

STUDY GUIDE

STASH IT IN YOUR HEART

Helping others, producing life, and nurturing relationships are the qualities each of us, as women, possess.

1. What do you think is the distinct purpose of being a woman?

    _____

    _____

    _____

2. What aspects of biblical womanhood are the hardest for you to embrace? Why?

    _____

    _____

    _____

3. Write a short description of how you can actively live out each pillar of biblical womanhood in your life today.

    _____

    _____

    _____

SHE HELPS OTHERS:_____

_____

_____

SHE PRODUCES LIFE: _____

_____

_____

SHE NURTURES RELATIONSHIPS: _____

_____

_____

Pray and ask God to help you put into action what you wrote down.

MAKE IT HAPPEN *Today*

Nurture a relationship. Send one encouraging note, text, or email to someone *today*.

7. OKAY, GIRLS, SHOW US HOW IT'S DONE

My grip was tight, my knees were slightly bent, and my toes were pointed toward the sky. "Okay . . . ready!" I (Bethany) yelled to the driver of the boat. The engine fired up, and within a matter of seconds I found myself looking like an underwater lure . . . again. This is me learning to wakeboard. I quickly learned that knowing and doing are two different things. After multiple tries and failures, I took a break. It wasn't until after I carefully watched my expert brother-in-law, Zack, that things clicked for me. I tried it again and finally succeeded.

Our hope is to show you how it's done so you can avoid becoming an underwater lure too.

Up until this point in the book, we've given you a lot of great information about biblical womanhood, but we haven't shown you how it works in real life. Instead of simply having you jump straight into the water, we want to give you real-life examples of biblical womanhood in action. Our hope is to show you how it's done so you can avoid becoming an underwater lure too.

First, we'll show you an unedited peek into our lives. We want you to see who we are beyond the pages of this book and how we're striving to live out biblical womanhood in our current stages of life.

Next, we'll peek inside the lives of two godly friends of ours who are also striving toward biblical womanhood in these modern days. These stories won't look exactly like yours, but they will show you this: regardless of your circumstances or background, you can live out God's design. Whether you're single or married, whether you do or don't have kids, each of the following real-life examples is filled with practical and encouraging takeaways.

I've realized that God's design is relevant to every woman in every stage of life.

First up, an engagement scene. Let's dive in.

Kristen

Stage of Life: Married, without Kids

With the sun setting on a cool Texas night, a handsome man knelt on one knee and asked me (Kristen) to be his wife. Without hesitation I said yes and pledged my heart and life to a godly man named Zack Clark. Eight long months later, I walked down the aisle at the age of twenty-four and made a lifelong covenant with my best friend.

After a refreshing and romantic honeymoon, we arrived back home in San Antonio to unwrap our gifts and turn our apartment into a home. We both understood and valued the second pillar of biblical womanhood (She Produces Life) and were open to having kids right away. Like any normal girl, I just assumed that if I didn't "prevent" pregnancy, then it would automatically happen. Right? Wrong. Little did I know that the next four years would consist of two unexpected miscarriages and a home distinctly void of a child's laughter.

Today, as I sit here and write these words, I am still childless. God has worked and reworked my heart to show me that being fruitful, producing life, and nurturing relationships comes in more forms than one.

During my single years, I had always imagined myself becoming a mom within the first two years of marriage. Obviously, things didn't go as I had planned, so I had to revamp my expectations. This unexpected season has broadened my view of biblical womanhood and helped me practice it in new and eye-opening ways. I've realized that God's design is relevant to every woman in every stage of life.

Even though I'm not a mom yet, I'm still a wife. Zack and I are lifelong teammates, and my goal is to consistently support and help him for the betterment of our family. I've learned that the role of a wife isn't equivalent to that of a housemaid. My responsibility as a helper, nurturer, and homemaker is crucial to our family. Actively embracing the Three Pillars of Biblical Womanhood has turned my house into a home.

Being a wife is so much more than planning nice dinners, keeping the house in order, running errands, and doing laundry. Yes, those things are important, but it's so much more than that. It's about getting on your knees every morning and becoming the biggest prayer warrior for the leader of your family. It's about fighting the lies of counterfeit femininity by creating a warm home environment in which relationships can thrive. It's about selflessly loving the man you pledged your life to and looking for ways to meet his needs. It's about displaying the gospel of Jesus Christ through the female and male roles. Contrary to the world's opinion, being a wife is so much more than being a roommate. As I've embraced my God-given role as a helper to Zack, my everyday tasks have taken on eternal significance. Being a wife is truly an indispensable role.

Saving money is a big deal for most young couples, so I've learned how to be a helper in the area of our finances. My DIY philosophy, such as learning to cut Zack's hair, highlighting my own hair, and sewing everything from curtains to skirts has saved us a ton of money. I'll also let you in on a little secret. I love getting my nails done—especially gel nail polish. But it can be pricey. So Zack surprised me several birthdays ago with an entire set of gel nail supplies (heat lamp and all). And get this—he watched online tutorials and learned how to do my nails himself! Not kidding. His tall stature and manly beard would never give away this secret.

Being a wife is truly an indispensable role.

In addition to saving money, I currently work part time at the Clark family business. It's a great way to engage in Zack's world, help him in the business, and bring in a little extra money. I also have the opportunity to work part time for my dad's family business, which is a fun way to stay connected with my own family.

Over the past few years, God has opened my eyes to the many opportunities I have experienced during this childless season. Producing spiritual life is something I've wholeheartedly pursued. Mentoring young women is a passion of mine and something I have time for. My time is also flexible right now, which enables me to focus more attention on GirlDefined Ministries by writing blog posts, interacting with young women, creating new material, speaking, etc. Being able to devote countless hours to *this* book is also a door God has opened for me.

Nurturing relationships through hospitality is also something Zack and I do on a regular basis. God has blessed us with a lovely home, so we open it up whenever we can. We regularly host dinners, parties, Bible studies, and overnight guests. My breakfast room has also evolved into the temporary office for GirlDefined Ministries. Bethany and I have spent many hours sitting at my breakfast table discussing ministry goals, writing blogs, and working on this book.

My life and actions aren't always perfect, but when I actively embrace biblical womanhood, my soul finds complete rest. When I take God at his word and value the things he values, I find real purpose. When I live out my womanhood for God's glory and not my own, even the mundane tasks of laundry and cleaning become meaningful.

God's Word has never failed me, and his design is the only thing that has given me lasting worth. The fulfillment, contentment, and joy that come from living God's way are undoubtedly worth it to me.

> *When I take God at his word and value the things he values, I find real purpose.*

Bethany

Stage of Life: Single, Living at Home

"I'm telling you, he would make great husband material," my friend said enthusiastically.

I (Bethany) laughed as she told me more about this "amazing" guy. I was being set up, again. Matchmaking talk is a fairly regular occurrence between me, my close friends, my mom, and my four sisters. When I was younger, I never thought I would still be single at my current age. Like Kristen, God had a very different plan for my early adult life than I had pictured.

I'm a girly girl who loves everything sparkly and shimmery. It isn't abnormal to find me in a puffy tulle skirt. Getting married to my Prince Charming by age twenty-one was my dream in high school. In fact, I thought my dream had come true when I met a fun, godly, and adventurous guy when I was nineteen. We totally hit it off, and I sincerely thought he was "the one." Well, to make a long story short, he wasn't the one. God closed that door through a series of eye-opening circumstances.

It took me a little while to recover from that heartbreak, but God gave me the grace to move on. I surrendered my dream of getting married young and asked God to help me accept his will for my life.

Pursuing a long-term career in the workforce was never a dream of mine, so I didn't follow the traditional college route. My passion was to be involved in some type of ministry. I tossed around the idea of going to Moody Bible College in Chicago, but God also closed that door. He made it very clear that staying in San Antonio was what I needed to do. I wanted to live out biblical womanhood during my single years but wasn't exactly sure how to do that.

After lots of prayer, biblical research, and wise counsel, God opened my eyes to exactly what I needed to do. My biggest ministry opportunities were right under my nose, and I couldn't even smell them. Instead of moving away from my home and my family to pursue something glamorous, God allowed me to serve and minister to the very people I was surrounded by. Sometimes following God is as simple as staying put. I also made the radical choice to remain living at home. I decided if I'm going to have roommates, I'd rather they be my family.

Sometimes following God is as simple as staying put.

As a result of my new realization, I began investing in the lives of my two youngest sisters, Rebekah and Suzanna, by mentoring them. I knew God wanted me to invest my time in producing spiritual life, and it wasn't an accident that God chose me to be the older sister. I put biblical womanhood to practice by nurturing my relationship with my sisters, as well as by mentoring other girls in my community. I also regularly host Bible studies for young women and have cohosted two different conferences.

During this season in my life (early twenties), I began to realize the value of my single years. I didn't have a husband, kids, or a house to look after, so my time was uniquely flexible. My mind-set took a 180-degree turn, and I began viewing my singleness as an extended blessing instead of a curse. With this new mind-set intact, I didn't want to waste any time. Sitting at home playing patty-cake until Prince Charming knocked on my door wasn't how I interpreted biblical womanhood. Being highly productive, intentional, and Christ-focused was the message I saw. And that's exactly how I wanted to live.

> *Sitting at home playing patty-cake until Prince Charming knocked on my door wasn't how I interpreted biblical womanhood.*

In addition to mentoring and hosting Bible studies, I became the director of my church's Awana program for elementary-aged girls. I also volunteered at my city's local pregnancy care center and served as a "big sister" to some young girls at a nearby public school. I'm not saying all of this to brag but simply to show you that being single has its perks. Single women can actively serve God by living out his design. Just like married women, single girls should actively build their lives on the Three Pillars of Biblical Womanhood.

As a single girl, I obviously don't have a husband to help yet, so I decided to assist my dad in his business. He had a need, and I was able to fill the position. This was a huge blessing to the business, and I gained some great work experience as a result. My job isn't always exciting and thrilling, but I've learned a valuable lesson: everything in life isn't a party; we do some things simply because they're the right thing to do. An added bonus is that my dad and I now have a much closer relationship as a result of spending so much time together. I know I'll never regret the time I've invested in his company.

More recently I've cut back on my office work to focus more time on GirlDefined Ministries and to write this book. Like Kristen, I spend a lot of time writing articles, brainstorming new content, speaking, and interacting with women. Let's just say I spend a lot of time in Kristen's breakfast room. I love it and am grateful for the opportunity to spread the message of God-defined femininity.

As I write these words, I'm still single. I'm entering my late twenties with no prospects in sight. And you know what? I have peace about it. Do I want to get married? Of course! Is it really hard for me at times? Absolutely. But I'm learning that God is in control of my life plans, and his ways are not my ways. His ways are better. Much better. He sees the bigger picture and knows exactly where I need to be. I pray for my future husband daily (hopeful that I will get married at some point) and trust that God will connect our lives when the timing is right.

God is in control of my life plans, and his ways are not my ways.

Until then, I'll continue to diligently serve God right where he has me.

Ashley

Stage of Life: College Graduate, Living on Her Own

Becoming involved in the pro-life movement has always been a passion of our lifelong friend Ashley, so, for her, law school seemed like a logical next step after college. After getting accepted into a prestigious law school, her dream opportunity was unfolding before her eyes.

As her first semester was coming to a close, the reality of her future hit her square between the eyes. Becoming a lawyer (and paying off the loans that would accompany the required degree) would take several years of intense, all-consuming study and work. Her future would be filled with traveling, long hours at the office, and paperwork that would leave her with little time for much else. Although being a lawyer sounded glamorous, she knew ultimately it wasn't the right career choice for her. The way she saw it, in order for her to practice law well and contribute meaningfully to the legal side of the pro-life debate, she would have to sacrifice many other desires.

She wanted to be a wife and a mom someday (sooner rather than later) and knew an intense career in law wouldn't leave adequate time for those other roles. As a lawyer, she wouldn't have the sort of time she wanted to invest in the lives of her future husband or kids. She would be a mom on the go, always busy, rarely available. Even though she would be fighting for a great cause, she strongly felt that being there for her family—which she wanted *more* than a demanding career—was most important. She understood the Three Pillars of Biblical Womanhood and knew it would be extremely stressful to be a successful wife, mom, and lawyer at the same time.

She didn't want to set her life on a course she would later regret.

After praying, seeking counseling, and studying God's Word for wisdom, Ashley chose to leave law school. She looked into her future with careful discernment and made a choice that would allow sufficient time and room for marriage and family.

Now, several years later, Ashley is grateful she made that choice. She still has plenty of opportunities to be politically involved in pro-life causes. They just look different and don't preclude her from *enjoying* the sort of family life she envisions. As a single gal living on her own, Ashley is a great example of a woman embracing biblical womanhood in her current season of life. She works full-time for a Christian organization, helping them advance their vision forward. She has developed the heart of a servant and does whatever is needed to help those she works with.

She doesn't let her small apartment stand in the way of nurturing relationships. With a sincere heart to honor God, she opens up her home by hosting many gatherings, parties, and dinners. She reaches out to others and invites them into her space on a regular basis.

Ashley understands the value of producing spiritual life in her current season, so she is actively involved in a great Bible study and intentionally makes efforts to get together with other women on a regular basis to encourage and edify them. She wholeheartedly embraces her God-given design and is willing to work hard to keep that her priority.

Emily

Stage of Life: Married, with Kids

"All right!" exclaimed the nurse. "Looks like you're having another boy." Emily's heart leaped with excitement.

"Another boy," she said softly with a huge smile. "That's great! Oh, how wonderful."

Emily had just entered her second trimester carrying baby number three. She already had a precious little boy and girl at home. She was married to her childhood sweetheart, Jared, and her life was turning out better than she could have imaged.

Prior to becoming a Christian during her senior year of high school, the thought of marriage and motherhood seemed extremely restricting to Emily. But as she began studying the Bible and reading every Christian book she could get a hold of, Emily's heart and mind began softening to the idea. She learned about biblical womanhood and understood how valuable the three pillars were in her life. She excitedly welcomed new life and viewed children as more than an accessory.

The responsibility to train, teach, and nurture her children was extremely important to both Emily and Jared. Life wasn't easy though. Jared's job barely made ends meet. Neither one wanted to put the babies in day care or get a nanny, so Emily brainstormed one night to figure out a way to meet their needs and desires.

After studying the Proverbs 31 woman and seeing how hardworking and ambitious she was, Emily had an idea. With Jared's support, Emily decided to open her own hair salon—right within the four walls of their garage. As a former stylist and cosmetology school graduate, Emily knew what she was doing.

She excitedly welcomed new life and viewed children as more than an accessory.

Within several months, Emily was bringing in enough money to help keep their budget in the black—and she was doing it from home! She scheduled her appointments during the kids' nap times and tried to maintain an orderly schedule. Things didn't always work out as planned, but she adjusted her days as needed. Regardless of what happened, though, her family's needs always came first.

By being flexible and creative, Emily was able to help her husband, nurture her children, and use her occupational training to bless her family and others.

Emily is busy. She doesn't have much time for outside ministry in this season of life, but as you can see, she's far from unproductive. She knows that time of raising little kids is short in the grand scheme of life, so she doesn't want to waste it. She doesn't want to look back on these days and wish she had poured more time into her family.

Emily knows how valuable her role is. She prays daily for her kids, teaches them Bible lessons, helps them memorize God's

Word, and models for them a godly character. Sure, a day care or nanny could fill the role of caretaker, but neither could fill the role of nurturer—at least not like she can. She is their God-ordained mom who alone was given these responsibilities.

> *She doesn't want to look back on these days wishing she had poured more time into her family.*

Although Emily's stage of life is very different from ours (Kristen and Bethany), she is pursuing the same foundational pillars in her life. She is investing time and energy into helping others, producing life, and nurturing relationships. One thing we particularly like about Emily is how she strategically combined her working skills with her home life. Her motivation was rooted in a servant's heart, and her intentions were to bless her husband and family.

What's Your Story?

We hope these real-life examples have encouraged your view of biblical womanhood. We hope you can see that God's design for the female isn't a cookie-cutter mold but one that all women in every stage of life can embrace. God's design transcends time and culture and is always relevant. Whether you're single, married, living on your own, or living at home with your parents, you can and should build your life on the Three Pillars of Biblical Womanhood.

Remember how the two of us went to the university and asked the question, "What is the purpose of being a girl?" Well, now you know the answer! God designed us, as women, to build our lives on the Three Pillars of Biblical Womanhood. Helping others, producing life, and nurturing relationships are foundational in our design. Women *are* different from men. By understanding and living out our feminine design, we bring immense glory to God. We show the world aspects of God's character that would not be displayed otherwise.

We have a question for you now. If your story was written in this book, what would it look like? We pray you will carefully consider what you've read in the past few chapters. God created you to be a female on purpose and for a purpose. May your womanhood no longer be about you but about living for the glory and honor of the One who designed you.

God's design transcends time and culture and is always relevant.

CHAPTER 7
STUDY GUIDE

STASH IT IN YOUR HEART

God's design for the female isn't a cookie-cutter mold but one that all women in every stage of life can embrace.

1. Which of the four women can you relate to the most? Why?

   _____

   _____

   _____

2. Write down three things that inspire you in these women's stories.

   1. _____

   2. _____

   3. _____

3. God's design for womanhood transcends time and culture and is _____ relevant.

   A. Never

   B. Sometimes

   C. Always

   D. Rarely

The correct answer is C. God's design is always relevant for every woman in every stage of life.

4. Pop quiz! Circle the Three Pillars of Biblical Womanhood and put an X on the Three Pillars of Counterfeit Femininity.

Sexual Freedom	Independence
Produces Life	Nurtures Relationships
Liberation	Helps Others

To check your answers, look at the bottom of the page.*

5. The four women in the stories from this chapter did not allow their age or season of life to hinder their productivity for God. What is hindering you from living out the Three Pillars of Biblical Womanhood? How can you overcome these hurdles?

MAKE IT HAPPEN *Today*

Practice hospitality today: Have some fun! Bake one dozen cookies (or your favorite dessert) and give them to someone who needs encouragement. Or make a homemade card and deliver it to a neighbor or friend.

---

*Three Pillars of Biblical Womanhood: Produces Life, Nurtures Relationships, and Helps Others. Three Pillars of Counterfeit Femininity: Sexual Freedom, Liberation, and Independence.

Part 3

WHEN IT COMES TO BEAUTY, TRUE LOVE, AND HARD WORK

8. BEAUTY THAT DOESN'T NEED A RUNWAY

Kylie Bisutti never imagined that only months after her nineteenth birthday she would become the number one googled person in the world.

Kylie was born in California but grew up in a small town called Jackpot, Nevada. Nothing in her life was unusual or special, except for one thing: Kylie was born with the body of a supermodel. She joined the modeling scene when she was fourteen years old. Over the next several years, she pursued many opportunities but never made it to the big leagues. As she grew older, she became discouraged with the modeling industry and questioned whether she wanted to be a part of it. As she pondered the direction of her future, she met an intriguing guy name Mike. It wasn't long before the two fell in love and were married.

Several months after the wedding, Kylie and Mike were visiting his parents when Kylie's new mother-in-law handed her a little card that would change her life forever. In bold letters she saw two little words that sparked her inner model: *Angel Search*.

Only days later Kylie was waiting in line, along with thousands of other girls, to try to win a spot in the 2009 Victoria's Secret Model Search. To her surprise, she beat the odds and made it past the first round. Before she had time to process what was happening, she found herself on a plane headed to New York City. Out of ten thousand girls, Kylie was chosen as one of only ten to compete in the final round.

After several weeks of competition, the votes were in. With nervous anticipation Kylie locked her eyes on the screen that would reveal the winner. After a long pause, the screen flashed. There before her eyes was her very own picture.

Kylie won the entire competition and fulfilled her lifelong dream of walking the runway in the Victoria's Secret Fashion Show. She had made it to the top. Kylie went from a nobody to an insanely famous supermodel overnight. Stardom and fame were her new reality.

The Big-Time Modeling Leagues

Being a famous supermodel seemed glamorous and romantic to Kylie until it became her reality. Winning the Victoria's Secret competition and walking the runway in the show left her with a public image she had to uphold. She was no longer just Kylie. She was Kylie the supermodel. She needed to look like the Kylie everyone saw on TV. No more running to the store without makeup on. No more leaving the house in sweatpants. In order for Kylie to look like "herself," she had to wear hair extensions, fake eyelashes, designer clothing, and loads of makeup everywhere she went.

Can you imagine living with that type of pressure? Think about it. Supermodels compete not only against thousands of other models but also against their own airbrushed image. Their entire success is based on one thing: their *outward appearance*.

After one year of living as a supermodel, Kylie had experienced enough. To the complete shock of the modeling world, she chose to end her modeling contract. By the grace of God, her eyes had been opened to the true value of her body and worth as a woman. She no longer felt the need to gain the acceptance and approval of others. She had no interest in showing off her body to the public. She was sick of being viewed as an object and not a real woman.

Kylie left her fame and status behind to pursue something much more fulfilling. "I quit being a VS model to be a Proverbs 31 wife,"[1] she said. Kylie no longer desired to be a supermodel. Instead, she wanted to be a godly role model. She realized that true beauty doesn't need a runway. Shortly after leaving the industry, she published a book titled *I'm No Angel: From Victoria's Secret Model to Role Model*.

In her book, Kylie discusses the intense preparations models go through to become "camera ready." She, along with other runway models, spent eight hours rotating between cosmetic prep stations. The models received spray tans, skin imperfection corrections, manicures, pedicures, hair extensions, lash extensions, layers of makeup, and so much more. It was hour after hour of full-body cosmetic transformation.

Kylie was considered one of the most gorgeous women on the planet, so why would she leave it all behind?

In Kylie's book, she openly details the constant struggles found in the modeling world. As I (Bethany) read her book, my eyes were opened (even wider) to just how icky the modeling world truly is. Kylie writes about how many of the models she knew either had dangerous dieting habits or suffered from anorexia or bulimia. Insecurity, depression, and unhappiness seemed to plague them as well.

Her drastic decision to end her career as a supermodel caused a lot of confusion in the public sphere. Kylie was considered one of the most gorgeous women on the planet, so why would she leave it all behind? Why would she give up the fame, attention, money, and stardom?

After reading Kylie's book and listening to several of her speaking sessions, I think I understand why she gave it up.

Pretty Girls Don't Have What It Takes

Many people assume that being drop-dead gorgeous must give a girl confidence and security. Kylie's experience proved the opposite. In a video interview, Kylie once said something to the effect that the top models she worked with were some of the most insecure women she's ever met (we read a quote earlier from Miranda Kerr, another supermodel, who said the same thing).[2] Both women were referring to some of the most flawless females on the planet. How can they be insecure? How can those women feel inadequate? They have the body every average girl dreams of. If those beauties are unhappy and insecure, shouldn't we, the average-bodied girls, be totally depressed?

Not necessarily.

Being "hot" or "average" isn't the determining factor for a woman's security and value. The truth is, whenever a woman bases her worth on what other people think of her, she will never measure up. No woman is perfect. No woman can ever adequately live up to the ideas and opinions of every person she

Kylie gave up the "dream" life to chase after something much more satisfying.

comes in contact with. No woman can wake up every day looking runway ready. It's unrealistic and impossible.

Kylie gave up the "dream" life to chase after something much more satisfying: using her life to point others to Christ.

When she made that radical turn from living for the approval of others to living for Christ, her sense of worth, security, and satisfaction shot through the roof. She had so much more confidence in who God created her to be. She no longer felt the need to please those around her. She no longer strove to win admiration from strangers. She no longer had to look perfect every time she stepped out her front door. She could finally fully accept and enjoy being the Kylie God designed her to be—imperfections and all.

Beauty Turned into the Beast

Humans have a history of placing a high importance on physical beauty, although the definition of what is beautiful varies from culture to culture. In America, the emphasis on appearance has become an intimidating beast. Beauty no longer feels like a gift from God but, rather, a living nightmare. The absurd expectations our culture puts on women are depressing and create an impossible reality.

Sadly, women have taken the bait. We've allowed the quest for beauty to become a scary, living thing that torments us day and night. *You aren't good enough. You'll never measure up. Look at that model on the magazine. She is the standard of beauty. No guy will ever love you. Your nose is too crooked. Look at those small lips. Ew, what an ugly mole.* On and on the taunting goes. We listen. We believe. We strive to measure up and please those around us. We fail. We become insecure and feel worthless. On and on the beast growls.

Instead of rejecting this beast, we have placed it on the altar of our hearts and worshiped it. We have made it an idol.

We may not bow down to a golden calf, but we do bow down to something. Elyse Fitzpatrick describes it perfectly in her book

Idols of the Heart. "Idols aren't just stone statues. No, idols are the thoughts, desires, longings, and expectations that we worship in the place of the true God. Idols cause us to ignore the true God in search of what we think we need."[3]

> *Beauty no longer feels like a gift from God but, rather, a living nightmare.*

That's exactly what many of us have done with beauty, isn't it? We ignore God and chase after external beauty in hopes of finding acceptance from others. We look in the mirror and think, *If only I were skinnier, then I'd be happy. If only I had bigger breasts, then I'd be happy. If only I were taller, then I'd be happy. If only that guy thought I was beautiful, then I'd be happy.*

I (Kristen) remember a time in my life when physical beauty was clearly an idol in my heart. I was convinced that if only I had (did you catch that—"*If only I had . . .?*") longer, thicker hair, then I'd be truly happy. I was sure if I had long locks, then I'd be the most confident, well-liked, secure woman around. I just needed the hair. Instead of laying my insecurities before God, I took matters into my own hands. Here's my story.

After several hours of research, I finally discovered the solution. Hair extensions! These weren't just any old hair extensions though. They were semipermanent hair extensions. Through one of my friends, I got connected with a woman who knew how to do things right. To make a long story short, I purchased real pieces of long blonde hair and this woman actually braided them in hidden rows underneath my hair. After she finished the last braid, I looked in the mirror.

I was stunned. My hair had instantly grown five inches longer and doubled in thickness. I finally had my dream hair! For the next few weeks, I walked with my head a little higher and felt a little prouder. I loved my new hair. I loved the extra glances and attention I received from guys when I went out in public. I was vain, and I didn't care.

Everything seemed to be going great for me until one unexpected evening. I had just finished showering and was lightly combing my fingers through my hair. I noticed that the braided hair underneath felt like it was knotting together. I tried to separate the braids, but they wouldn't come apart. I called in some reinforcements for help. My mom came upstairs and gently tried to separate my braids. Nothing was budging. I began to panic slightly.

"Okay," my mom said calmly. "I think we should try to take out the extensions."

"My extensions?" I exclaimed. "Oh no . . ."

I didn't want to lose my beautiful hair. After several hours of trying to get this massive knot out, I finally agreed. My mom began undoing the smallest part of the braids and sliding the extensions off. One by one my vanity hit the floor.

"You still have a really large knot in your hair, Kris," my mom said slowly. "Let's try to gently brush it out."

My mom worked for several more hours, but the giant knot didn't budge a bit. I'm not exaggerating this story at all. We searched the internet for help and tried everything from oil to mayonnaise to wrapping my hair in plastic wrap. Nothing worked. Then I hit the breaking point. Tears burst from my eyes as I realized the only possible outcome. My mom would have to cut this giant knot (three inches across!) out of my hair. I was about to lose one-third of my regular hair. My face was red from crying as my mom gently snipped the horrible nightmare from my head. As a result of my vanity, I ended up with less hair than I started with.

I loved the extra glances and attention I received from guys when I went out in public.

I vowed never again to get hair extensions. In fact, I wished with all my heart that I could go back in time and change my decision to get them in the first place.

A Hard but Valuable Lesson

Clearly, the hair extensions weren't my problem. Beauty had become an idol in my life. My attention had shifted from being Christ-focused to being self-focused. I assumed that if I could fix what I didn't like about my outward appearance, then I would be truly happy. Boy was I wrong. As Proverbs 11:2 says, "When pride comes, then comes disgrace, but with the humble is wisdom."

I learned two valuable lessons the day my vanity fell to the floor.

LESSON #1: Wanting beautiful hair (or whatever your desire is) isn't the problem. The problem takes root when that thing becomes the means to finding or measuring your worth, value, and acceptance.

LESSON #2: A woman will feel content with her physical appearance only when she stops basing her worth and value on what others think of her and, instead, starts living to please Christ.

One of the biggest reasons we, as women, feel insecure with our physical appearance is because we take our eyes off Christ only to place them on ourselves. We become self-focused instead of Christ-focused. That is the root of all insecurities. The crazy thing is that we often do this without even realizing it. Thanks to our sinful hearts, we're constantly battling against our flesh, which loves being consumed with *self*. "For all that is in the world—the desires of the flesh and the desires of the eyes and pride of life—is not from the Father but is from the world" (1 John 2:16).

For example, you're innocently going about your day and feeling pretty good, but then you look in the mirror and see something you don't like—*wham!* Your focus instantly zooms in on yourself. You lose sight of the fact that Christ is the only One who can satisfy you (Prov. 19:23). You forget that he is the only One who can fill your affirmation tank. So . . . you begin to feel insecure.

In those moments, you have to intentionally refocus your heart on Christ. You have to consciously deny your flesh and say no to the lies. How do you do that? By speaking truth to yourself. Instead of getting wrapped up in a self-pity party, you must realign your heart with God's truth.

The best way to do that is by reminding yourself of what God says. Matthew 6:33 is a great place to start: "But seek first the kingdom of God and his righteousness, and all these things will be added to you." Or Psalm 37:4, "Delight yourself in the LORD, and he will give you the desires of your heart." Another great verse to quote is Psalm 103:1–2, "Bless the LORD, O my soul, and all that is within me, bless his holy name! Bless the LORD, O my soul, and forget not all his benefits."

Instead of getting wrapped up in a self-pity party, you must realign your heart with God's truth.

You must remind yourself that no amount of beauty, compliments, or popularity can replace the fulfillment you find in your relationship with Christ. As Kylie learned, being drop-dead gorgeous on the outside can't bring a woman lasting fulfillment and security on the inside. Those things are found only when a woman chooses to base her value in what Christ thinks of her and not in what the world thinks.

THE PROBLEM: Insecurity results from self-focusedness.

The Solution: Security results from Christ-focusedness.

Get Rid of the Beast

Physical beauty does not have to be a beast. It is an amazing gift from God that should be enjoyed by both men and women and, when viewed from a biblical perspective, can be fun and enjoyable.

We (Kristen and Bethany) enjoy dressing fashionable and feminine. We both enjoy doing our hair and makeup on a regular basis. We like enhancing the natural facial features God has given us. We enjoy exploring new products to see what works and what doesn't. When our security and happiness isn't based on our outward appearance, these things can be fun without becoming idols. We can get dressed in the morning, take a quick glance in the mirror, and enjoy the rest of our day without worrying what others think of us. Our security is found in Christ, which results in us being able to enjoy God's gift of beauty.

On the flip side, we'll be the first to admit we're not perfect. We're tempted by the beast just like you. Each of us has specific things about our physical appearance that we don't always love. For example, I (Kristen) have been really ungrateful for my nose at times. I compare its shape to other people's noses and wish it were a little thinner. This is one area I have to intentionally surrender to God. Also, I (Bethany) have been through a lot with my teeth. I wore braces for six years but was not happy with the outcome. However, my smile is the best it can be. This has been an area of discontentment for me at times. I have to remind myself to thank God for the teeth I do have instead of complaining about what I don't have.

We've learned it doesn't matter what culture portrays as the ideal woman. It only matters what Christ thinks. This verse has given both of us comfort: "For you formed my inward parts; you knitted me together in my mother's womb. I praise you, for I am fearfully and wonderfully made. Wonderful are your works; my soul knows it very well" (Ps. 139:13–14).

God designed you to look just the way you do. He handcrafted your body with intention and love. Allow your soul to echo the words of the psalmist, "Wonderful are your works; my soul knows it very well!"

God designed you to look just the way you do.

The moment you take your eyes off yourself and put them on Christ, your heart will be content with your physical appearance because you're living to please him. It's not magic. It's not complicated. It's really rather simple. Look to Christ. And when you do, the beast will fade into the background, and your life will be filled with true beauty and lasting security, gratitude, and confidence.

CHAPTER 8

STUDY GUIDE

STASH IT IN YOUR HEART

A woman will feel content with her physical appearance only when she stops basing her worth and value on what others think of her and, instead, starts living to please Christ.

1. Have you ever wished you looked more like a supermodel? If so, why did you wish that?

   _____

   _____

   _____

2. When it comes to your outward appearance, what are your "If only I hads . . .?" What physical features do you wish looked different? Customize the following blanks:

   If only I had _____ then I'd be happy.

   If only I had _____ then I'd be happy.

   If only I had _____ then I'd be happy.

   If only I had _____ then I'd be happy.

   After reading this chapter, do you still believe that receiving the things you wrote above will truly make you happy?

3. Circle the words that best reflect your feelings regarding your physical appearance:

Ingratitude	Security
Insecurity	Gratitude
Worthlessness	Confidence

According to your answers, are you more like Woman #1 or Woman #2?

WOMAN #1: Her heart is rooted in self-focusedness. She struggles with ingratitude, insecurity, and worthlessness. She has an idol in her heart of wanting to please others more than God.

WOMAN #2: Her heart is rooted in Christ-focusedness. She is overflowing with security, gratitude, and confidence. Her heart is content with how God designed her, and she lives her life to please him.

4. Instead of complaining about the "If only I hads," it's time to express gratitude to God. In the blanks below, write down features of your body that you have never thanked God for.

Thank you God for creating my _____

Thank you God for giving me _____

Thank you God for _____

Thank you God that I have _____

5. Do you truly believe what Psalm 139:13–14 says? Meditate on these verses whenever you're feeling discontent: "For you formed my inward parts; you knitted me together in my mother's womb. I praise you, for I am fearfully and wonderfully made. Wonderful are your works; my soul knows it very well."

Which mirror do you use the most in your house? Go to that mirror and write this on it (use a dry erase marker, lipstick, toothpaste, or whatever you can find that will easily wipe off): "For you, O LORD, have made me glad by your work; at the works of your hands I sing for joy" (Ps. 92:4).

9. WHEN TRUE LOVE AND FEMININITY COLLIDE

I (Bethany) sat in awe as I watched the princess in disguise run from the palace guards. She was sick of her dull life and of being stuck all alone in her big, boring castle. She wanted adventure. She wanted excitement. She wanted romance.

My little nine-year-old self was completely captivated by the beautiful princess and her daring quest for freedom and romance. The princess soon found true love, swooning in the strong arms of a handsome local boy as he rescued her from the palace guards. My heart pounded as I watched the boy finish the enchanting day off with nothing less than a magic carpet ride through the twinkling night sky.

Without even realizing it, my little brain was taking big notes. My view of love and romance was subtly being shaped by the culture around me. As the years went on, I began forming a running checklist of what true love looked like. I imagined my future husband to be physically gorgeous and practically perfect in every way. He would be my knight in shining armor. My prince to the rescue. My happiness maker. He would love me unconditionally and accept me for who I am. He would jump at the chance to bring me flowers. He would always want to hold my hand. He would treat me like a queen. And, of course, my happiness would be his number one priority.

Wow. Should we all laugh out loud? Obviously, my view of true love hadn't collided with reality yet. Although most of us would agree that the perfect man doesn't exist, we are often unaware of how much culture has influenced our view of love and romance.

When we were little girls, the Disney movies we watched sent the message that we'd find true love complete with a handsome rescuer and a happily-ever-after ending. Then we became teenagers and thought true love was as simple as butterflies, crushes, and late-night messaging. Once we grew into adults, true love looked more like finding a man who would meet all our needs and constantly make us happy.

My view of love and romance was subtly being shaped by the culture around me.

From secular magazines to movies to reality TV shows to music, we are fed the same underlying message about love. It goes something like this: true love is about *you* finding someone who will make *you* happy because *you* deserve it.

In doing research for this chapter, we came across an article titled: "16 Signs It's Time to Move On and End the Relationship."[1] In this article, the number one sign for ending the relationship was . . . drumroll please . . . "The spark is missing." Basically, when the fireworks end, the relationship is dead. Why stick around?

Sadly, many Christian women have bought into this way of thinking. In fact, conservative Christian women have been duped too. I (Kristen) am a living example of that. I wouldn't have said it, but early in my marriage, I looked to Zack to always make me happy. He would be the man who would lead me perfectly and never fail me. My view of love was largely centered around one thing—*me*.

In addition to embracing a self-centered view of love, modern women are encouraged to discard any traces of biblical femininity and masculinity from their relationships. Have you ever heard/seen quotes like these? "I'm not a princess. I'm a queen. I can handle things on my own" or "Don't be a woman who needs a man. Be a woman who a man needs."

The overall message is clear: become a "strong" woman who can take or leave a man as you choose. A biblical definition of femininity and masculinity play little to no role in the relationship.

As a result of our culture's self-centered view of love and lack of God-defined gender roles, everyone (including Christians) is suffering when it comes to romantic relationships.

An article by the *Daily Mail* stated that the average woman will kiss fifteen men, enjoy two long-term relationships and have her heart broken twice.[2] If that isn't bad enough, further statistics show that around 40 percent of all marriages end in divorce.[3]

The truth is that we don't need statistics and studies to show us how unsuccessful relationships are. Just look around. How many struggling marriages do you see? How many dysfunctional relationships have you experienced? How many divorces have you watched unfold? The elephant in the room is screaming at us, "Something isn't working!" and it's time we opened our eyes and paid attention.

Unless we, as Christian women, break free from this distorted view of love and gender roles, we will all end up sinking in the same miserable boat.

Defining True Love

The word *love* comes in all shapes and sizes. We use it in a casual moment after we bite into a hot slice of pizza or in a monumental moment as we stand at the altar on our wedding day. *Love.* Such a short but powerful word. Most of us use the word *love* when we're feeling happy. When the object or person in front of us is making life better.

Romantic love takes things a step further. It's usually portrayed as a powerful emotion that overtakes you and hijacks your brain. Sparks fly and fireworks explode. True love has arrived.

The word love comes in all shapes and sizes.

Is this really what love is though? The result of a happy emotion? The tingling feeling in your stomach? While those things are great and can be a result of love, they're not the definition of love. And that's right where mainstream society gets confused. Most romantic relationships and marriages are built on the belief that true love should always create happy feelings. Once the happy feelings are gone, love must be gone too. Right? So what happens? The couple breaks up or gets divorced.

If we want better results for our romantic relationships, then we have to get to the root of what true love is. We have to build our relationships on a strong foundation of God-defined love.

God-defined love is the polar opposite of most everything we see in our secular society. Why? Because it goes against every fiber in our beings. It runs completely contrary to our self-centered hearts. "For the flesh desires what is contrary to the Spirit" (Gal. 5:17 NIV).

Do you know what the most commonly used Greek word for love is in the Bible? Pop quiz time!

A. EROS
B. AGAPE
C. PHILEO

Did you pick *agape*? If so, nice job! The Greek word *agape* is mentioned 259 times in the New Testament. If the Bible repeats something 259 times, we should pay attention.

When we break down the original meaning of this word, its definition is earth-shattering. Are you ready for it? Here it is: *The essence of agape love is self-sacrifice.* Did you catch that last part? *Self-sacrifice.* Ouch.

Isn't it interesting how much we, as humans, like the word *self* when it stands alone, but when it's tacked onto a word like *sacrifice* we begin to cringe?

God-defined love isn't built on self but, rather, on a foundation of sacrifice. Love is an action, not a feeling (1 Cor. 13). *Self-sacrifice* is the action that best displays true, biblical love.

The real-life story of Ian and Larissa Murphy displays *agape* love in a powerful way.

Maybe you've seen their website or on-line videos. If not, here's a summary of their story: They were young and in love. Their entire future was ahead of them. Everything seemed perfect in their lives, and Ian couldn't wait to propose to Larissa. Then suddenly, without any warning, something drastic changed their lives *forever.* Ian was involved in a head-on car collision. His body was crushed. His brain was damaged.

God-defined love is the polar opposite of most everything we see in our secular society.

Against all odds, Ian survived the terrible accident, but his brain would never be the same. He could no longer function independently.

Instead of deserting Ian because of his serious brain injury, Larissa did something surprising. She married him. She abandoned her dreams of a "perfect life" and, instead, chose to sacrificially serve the man she loved.[4]

True love. That's it. Right there. Larissa chose self-sacrifice over self-pleasure. She put true love into *action.* Sure, their marriage has been really difficult at times. Sure, she hasn't always been totally happy, but she is devoted. True love doesn't crumble when life gets tough—it perseveres.

I (Kristen) love how this quote describes it: "Love is best seen as devotion and action, not an emotion. Love is not exclusively based on how we feel. Certainly our emotions are involved, but they cannot be our only criteria for love. True devotion will always lead to action—true love."[5]

Love is an action, not a feeling.

We must allow God to define our view of love. Christ was the ultimate example of sacrificial love, and he calls us to love others in the same way. "Therefore be imitators of God, as beloved children. And walk in love [*agape*], as Christ loved us and gave himself up for us, a fragrant offering and sacrifice to God" (Eph. 5:1–2).

Whether married or single, *agape* love is God's solution for vibrant, lasting relationships.

Good Old-Fashioned Romance

His strong arms reached up to help her down. "Why, thank you, kind sir," she said, a twinkle in her blue eyes. Grabbing her long skirt, she carefully exited the coach.

"May I escort you inside?" he asked, straightening his suit jacket.

"Yes . . . that would be lovely," she said with a smile.

With her slender arm linked in his, he led her down the stairs and into the opulent mansion.

Romance. You can smell it a mile away. Despite the fact that we no longer live in the 1800s, old-fashioned romance still intrigues many of us. Modern women are drawn to books and movies that distinguish the pursuer from the one being pursued and in which innocent courtships take place and traditional families remain strong. And you know what? There's something we like about that.

In contrast, modern romances have thrown the "relationship rulebook" in the trash. Today either gender can initiate the relationship. Either can be the pursuer. Either can do the proposal. Sex is tossed around like a toy. Purity is a joke. Women are aggressive. Men are passive. Traditional families are being replaced with progressive ones. Gender roles are close to extinct. Although some might view these things as accomplishments, the results

True love doesn't crumble when life gets tough — it perseveres.

are nothing short of devastating (as we mentioned before, just look around and you'll see the brokenness). Instead of leaving our feminine design at the door, we need to carry it into our romantic relationships. Why? Because God created us to be women for a reason. True success comes from welcoming God's design in every area of our lives.

Why Gender Roles Matter

So what does it look like to welcome God's design into our romantic relationships? Like we mentioned in chapter 5, God created males and females to have different but equally valuable roles. When it comes to romance, gender matters. A lot! Although the Bible doesn't give us a cookie-cutter guide for how every romantic relationship should play out, it does give us principles for how our gender roles should guide the relationship. Since the man is created to be the leader, this clues us in on who should be the initiator and pursuer in the relationship. Since the woman is created to be the helper, this clues us in on who should be the responder.

Check out the way John Piper describes our differing roles:

> At the heart of mature masculinity is a sense of benevolent responsibility to lead, provide for and protect women in ways appropriate to a man's differing relationships. At the heart of

mature femininity is a freeing disposition to affirm, receive and nurture strength and leadership from worthy men in ways appropriate to a woman's differing relationships.[6]

Whether you're married, single, or in a relationship, these truths should affect the way you view romantic relationships. When you welcome God's design for gender roles into your romantic relationship, you will help set up you and your husband (or boyfriend) for long-term success.

Scoot Over and Let Him Lead

One of the biggest complaints we hear from Christian women (single and married) about men is that they won't lead. They won't initiate. They won't be *men*. Ever said that? While it's not our responsibility for how a man behaves, there are a lot of things we can do to encourage godly leadership. Our actions have a powerful influence over men. The way we act, speak, dress, and behave has the ability to (1) encourage godly masculinity and leadership or (2) encourage passivity and complacency.

In contrast, modern romances have thrown the "relationship rulebook" in the trash.

A headstrong Christian woman named Heidi learned this the hard way. Take a look at this story from Mary A. Kassian's *Girls Gone Wise in a World Gone Wild*:

> She saw a guy she liked. She asked him out. She insisted on paying for half their dates. She called him. She kissed him. She brought up the subject of marriage. She negotiated the terms. She insisted on a hyphenated name. She made him give up his job and move because of hers. She made more money, so she made him stay home with the kids. OK. Now fast-forward ten years into their relationship:

136

Heidi hates her husband. Her complaint? He's unmotivated. A deadweight. She has to beg him to do anything. He doesn't initiate. He's wimpy, whiny, and disgusting. She's the only one contributing. And she's exhausted.

Wait a minute, Heidi. Let me get this straight: You asked him out. You pursued him. You took the lead. You dominated the relationship. Like putty in your hand, you molded him into what you wanted him to be . . . and now you hate him for it? What's more you expect him to go against years of emasculation and suddenly become a man? Why should he? You're the "man" in your house—or at least you pretended that you could be.[7]

Women dominating the leadership have landed thousands of relationships and marriages right where Heidi is.

Calling Out the Hero in Your Man

If we want better results from our romantic relationships, we need a better course of action. Instead of using our feminine strength to dominate, let's channel our influence in a direction that will actually encourage men to be men!

Whether you're single, in a relationship, or married, learning how to promote godly manhood is key to a successful relationship. In addition to showing *agape* (sacrificial) love, here are some practical things you can do to encourage godly manhood in your husband or boyfriend:

> *Let's channel our influence in a direction that will actually encourage men to be men!*

1. ENCOURAGE HIS LEADERSHIP (1 COR. 11:3). If you're interested in dating someone, wait for him to ask you out. Wait for him to make his own moves. In any relationship, ask him what he thinks and listen. Allow him to make decisions in the

relationship. Ask for his advice on small and big things. Affirm him when he makes a good decision, even if it's a simple one.

2. SPEAK WORDS OF LIFE (PROV. 16:24). Strive to remove negative language from your vocabulary. Instead, choose powerful words of encouragement. Call out the good in your man. Praise his godly character, thoughts, and actions.

3. HELP HIM SUCCEED (GEN. 2:18). Help your man succeed as he strives to be the leader and provider. Take an interest in his occupation. Affirm his accomplishments and show that you are supportive and available to listen.

4. LET HIM BE STRONG (1 COR. 16:13-14; 1 PETER 3:7). Encourage his God-given masculinity in every way possible. Allow him to protect you. Ask him to escort you through a crowded restaurant or event. If he's able, let him open doors for you.

5. ENCOURAGE SPIRITUAL LEADERSHIP (EPH. 5:25-26). This is huge! For many Christian women, having a man who can lead her spiritually is high on the list. Pray for him daily. Send him uplifting notes and verses during the week. Ask his opinion on spiritual matters. Pray daily that God would raise him up to be a man who loves the Lord and the Bible.

The more you embrace your God-defined womanhood, the more you will encourage your man to rise to the occasion. The most powerful way you can promote godly masculinity is to live out godly femininity.

Use Your Femininity to Promote Purity

One of the most impactful ways to cultivate a successful relationship is to use your femininity to promote moral purity. Moral purity will help you not only avoid heartache and misery but also honor the God who created you.

By God's strength, both Zack and I (Kristen) remained virgins until our wedding night. The reward of saving sexual intimacy for each other is something we will always cherish and never regret.

Whether you're married or single, God calls you to a life of moral purity (1 Thess. 4:3–5). If you've blown it in the past, it's not too late to change. From this point forward, you can promote purity in your relationship.

A Letter to the Unmarried Girls (from Bethany)

Hey, girl. Being single isn't easy. Having a boyfriend isn't easy either. The sexual temptations are relentless—for both us and our brothers in Christ. To cultivate purity in our romantic relationships, we need to aggressively pursue hearts and minds of purity before God.

Personally, I do this by getting rid of the garbage (unhealthy magazines, movies, websites, etc.) in my life and replacing it with material that will feed my soul. Reading God's Word every day is a great place to start. Also, pick a few verses to memorize, and meditate on them every time you're tempted. I like Psalm 51:10, which says, "Create in me a pure heart, O God, and renew a steadfast spirit within me" (NIV). Read solid Christian books* that will fill your mind with the right messages.

Once your heart is right, look for ways to help your brothers in Christ achieve purity. Don't allow your personal desire for physical closeness to drag your relationship down the wrong road. Exercise self-control in how much you touch him. Dress in a way that draws attention to your face rather than your curves. Use discretion regarding the movies and TV shows you watch together.

It's unlikely that you will regret having been "too pure." I pray you will join me in the fight for purity. May your romantic

*Like this one. *wink*

relationship(s) be marked by God's character and design for marriage.

Love, Bethany

A Letter to the Married Girls (from Kristen)

Hey, married gal. Let's pretend we're chatting in a coffee shop. Okay, you and I both know that many people don't view marriage as a lifelong covenant anymore, so it's not protected quite as fiercely. If we want more for our marriages, we'd better fight a lot harder. Purity is just as important after marriage as it is before.

Zack and I fight for our marriage by setting up boundaries and guardrails of protection. Here are some of the things I do to safeguard my heart. For example, I never flirt with other men, even on social media sites. This is a slippery slope that never leads in a good direction. I am intentionally never alone with one man (in a room, car, etc.). Although this might sound extreme, my goal is to create a large buffer between me and the first step of compromise.

Personally, I've found that romance novels create a heart of impurity and discontentment in me, so I don't read those anymore. Another thing I strive not to do—and highly encourage you not to do as well—is this: don't ever compare your marriage to someone else's, and especially don't compare your husband to other men. This creates a heart of dissatisfaction and opens the door for Satan to walk right in and destroy your marriage.

On the flip side, one positive thing I do to strengthen my marriage is to pray for my husband every day. I spend time lifting up Zack in prayer and asking God to protect our marriage and give Zack wisdom to be a godly leader. Prayer is a powerful tool God enables us to use every day (1 John 5:14–15). Zack and I also pray together as a couple every morning and every evening. Sometimes the prayers are short and sweet, but they consistently turn our focus heavenward.

My marriage with Zack isn't perfect, but by God's strength we're fighting as hard as we can to protect it.

Girl, we're in this battle together. Let's be wives who never grow tired of fiercely protecting our marriages.

XOXO, *Kristen*

Lifetime Love Is Possible

Romantic love can be the sweetest or the sourest thing you taste depending on how you approach it. The world's ideas sound and look good, but they don't end well. God's way requires sacrifice, patience, and faith in his design but will produce vastly better results. Be the woman who inspires change in others through your obedience to God.

For wives, true love isn't about getting all your needs met. Rather, it's about selflessly loving your man for the glory and honor of Christ. For unmarried, be picky and careful. Don't rush into a romantic relationship without a lot of prayer and wise counsel. Look for a man who loves the Lord and desires to honor him with his life.

> *Be the woman who inspires change in others through your obedience to God.*

We, as women, can have so much hope for our romantic relationships if we do things God's way. As Sheila Gregoire says so well, "In a world of celebrities constantly splitting up, having a good, solid marriage is something that can make others believe that God does make a difference, and that lifetime love is possible."[8]

CHAPTER 9
STUDY GUIDE

God-defined love isn't built on self but, rather, on a foundation of sacrifice. Love is an action, not an emotional feeling.

1. In what ways has Hollywood's version of love influenced your thinking?

    _____

    _____

    _____

2. For single girls: What expectations are you placing on your future relationship to make you happy? How has culture's self-centered version of love influenced your expectations?

    _____

    _____

    _____

3. For married girls: What expectations are you currently placing on your husband to make you happy? How has culture's self-centered version of love influenced your expectations?

    _____

    _____

    _____

4. The essence of *agape* love is self-sacrifice. Is your love built on self-sacrifice? Write down one paragraph on how you can show *agape* love today.

_____

_____

_____

5. How can you apply each of these five actions to your relationship with your husband or boyfriend (or in a future relationship)? Write down one idea under each:

- Encourage his leadership.

_____

- Speak words of life.

_____

- Help him succeed.

_____

- Let him be strong.

_____

- Encourage spiritual leadership.

_____

6. Whether you're married or single, are you actively promoting purity in your life? What changes do you need to make to honor God in this area?

_____

_____

_____

MAKE IT HAPPEN *Today*

Question number 5 on the previous page lists five ways you can encourage the man in your life (for single girls, you can practice on your dad, brother, etc.). Pick one of those five areas and put it into action *today.*

10. HARDWORKING WOMEN DOIN' IT RIGHT

I (Kristen) glanced around the table, feeling out of place as I was surrounded by successful doctors, wealthy business owners, and men and women who made a lot of money. I was attending a business dinner with my husband for his company. These people were highly successful according to the world's standards. In fact, I'm pretty sure my car cost less than their jewelry. I picked up my water glass and casually took a sip, trying to look comfortable. The truth is I wanted to be anywhere else but at *that* table. As a get-to-know-one-another conversation began and then progressed, I felt even smaller.

Suddenly, the dreaded moment arrived.

"What do you do, dear?" a retired female doctor asked, looking directly at me. All eyes turned in my direction. My tongue went dry. I smiled and then hesitated, trying to think of something good to say. Nothing came.

"I . . . I just work for my husband's business and run a ministry for Christian girls and women," I said half apologetically.

"Oh, interesting," she replied sweetly.

Conversation over.

I wanted to sink into the floor and disappear. My life's work looked pathetic compared to what she had accomplished. I was extremely grateful when the night ended.

You can probably relate to my feelings on some level. We live in a society that equates a person's success with how much money they have, whether their business is prosperous, or how prestigious their career is. The pressure to become "someone" is pushed on us the moment we're old enough to get a job.

The pressure to become "someone" is pushed on us the moment we're old enough to get a job.

We (Kristen and Bethany) constantly wrestled with this pressure after high school and, to be honest, still do at times. Everywhere we turned, we felt the pressure to measure up to other people's definition of success. Deep down, we wanted to be praised and admired by those around us. We wanted to look successful in the world's eyes. We wanted to spout off some elaborate answer when people asked us the dreaded question, "What are you doing with your life?" Can you relate to us here? Whether you're approaching your twenties or well past them, you've probably felt the pressure we're talking about.

As the two of us struggled and prayed through what to do with our lives, one question kept popping into our minds: "What does it mean to be a successful woman?" Honestly, we weren't sure how to answer that question. What we didn't realize then, but do now, is that the answer to that question is the driving force for why any woman does what she does.

Rubbing Elbows in the Corporate World

Most women want to be viewed as successful. Don't you? Well, depending on your definition of a successful woman, you will be driven

146

to pursue success according to that belief. The reality is that most of us don't have a strong definition of what it means to be biblically successful, so we default to the most popular opinion out there.

I (Bethany) did an internet search to get an idea of how culture defines a woman as successful. I typed in the question, "What is a successful woman?" and clicked on the image tab. Pictures are worth a thousands words, right? Within a matter of seconds, my computer screen was filled with images of women wearing suit jackets, women giving presentations, women in board meetings, and women working on their computers.

The message I received was pretty clear: A successful woman in the twenty-first century works in the corporate world. She rubs elbows with men and women in prestigious business meetings. She is quickly climbing the corporate ladder.

Most women want to be viewed as successful.

A popular Forbes article titled "The World's Most Inspiring Women"[1] revealed the magazine's list of female role models. The list contained a well-known journalist, a novelist, a supermodel, a race car driver (who shows that "females are just as fast as men"), and an elderly actress who was praised for her bravery in posing nude, among others.

The theme of this article made it pretty clear that the measure of a woman's success is almost entirely linked to one thing: her career. Author and Bible teacher Nancy DeMoss Wolgemuth stated that it appears that "the identity and value of women has come to be equated with their role in the community or in the marketplace. That is how their 'worth' is generally defined, measured, and experienced."[2]

Whether or not you like it, in twenty-first-century society a woman's job is the standard for measuring her success. We're told to "get out there and work" so we can build our independence, become self-sufficient, embrace our liberation, and further our personal careers. As a result of this popular push, many Christian women have adopted this worldview and pursue success according to this belief.

This belief drives women to prioritize their careers as the most important part of their lives. By default, they dedicate the largest chunk of their time, energy, and effort to being successful according to culture's definition.

As popular as this definition may be, it poses two major problems for us as Christian women because (1) it leaves God completely out of the picture, and (2) it is always *changing*.

The Forever-Changing Standard

What is normal today wasn't normal one hundred years ago. The women who lived a century ago were measured by a completely different standard for success than the women of today. As the economy continually changes, so does the measurement for a woman's success. In fact, if you traveled around the world today, you would discover that each individual culture has a slightly different standard for measuring a woman's success.

The same goes for past cultures. Think of the women in the Old Testament. What was the culture's standard for a successful woman? Hint: It wasn't a race car driver. They measured a woman's success based on how many sons she could bear. Remember Rachel? "Give me children, or I shall die!" (Gen. 30:1).

Culture's definition of success is always changing.

This goes to show us that culture's definition of success is always changing. It's continually evolving. The pressures our daughters will face will be different from the pressures we face. This reality poses a dilemma for us. Why? Because an ever-evolving standard is an *unreliable* standard.

If we, as Christian women, want to be truly successful, we have to build our lives on a reliable, unchanging standard. And the only standard that never changes is the one we find in the Bible. God's Word is rock solid. And it doesn't leave us guessing when it comes to the topic of work either. God clearly lays out his principles for work and his priorities for women. In fact, he is one of the biggest promoters of hard work, ambition, and productivity.

Let's explore what God's Word says about women, work, and what it means to be truly successful.

Hardworkin' Women

With the sun peeking through her window, she knew she had to hurry. Strapping on her sandals and grabbing her bag, she rushed out for another day of work. She waved to the other women as she entered the gate. Kneeling down in the corner, she began another long day of gathering wheat in the field. As the day progressed, her face became dirty, her clothes became sweaty, and she smelled a little stinky. This woman knew how to work hard.

A different woman experienced a similar routine, only her days were filled with cutting fabric and tying rope. This woman spent her days working hard in the sun alongside her husband, advancing her family's tentmaking business. She knew how to work hard too.

A third woman pursued a much different job. She was a skilled merchant, known for her high-quality fabrics and rich colors. She worked with her hands, dying cloth and creating colorful fabrics fit for a king. People came from all over the country to buy her handcrafted work. This woman knew how to work hard.

These biblical women knew the value of hard work and ambition.

Who are these three hardworking women? They're none other than Ruth, Priscilla, and Lydia from the pages of the Bible. As you probably know, Ruth worked in a field (Ruth 2), Priscilla was a tentmaker (Acts 18), and Lydia was a seller of purple cloth (Acts 16). These biblical women knew the value of hard work and ambition, but they also knew the secret to God-defined success.

Before you read any further, we want you to make a deal with the two of us. For the rest of this chapter, you have to drop all your preconceived ideas about success. For just a moment, set aside your personal opinions and let God speak to your heart. In fact, why don't you stop and pray? Simply ask God to soften your heart to his version of a successful woman. That's it. Go for it.

It's Not about Knitting Socks

When the two of us scoured our Bibles for answers to our questions about what kind of work to pursue in our lives, we made some eye-opening discoveries. We examined the lives of godly women throughout the pages of Scripture and found some astonishing results. The women in the Bible weren't sitting around knitting socks morning till night—they were working hard! *Really* hard. They were ambitious go-getters who loved God. We liked that.

As we studied even further, we realized that hard work was a part of God's perfect plan from the beginning of time. Hard work is a good and godly thing. Before sin entered the world, Adam and Eve were given dominion over the entire earth and called to work hard on the land (Gen. 1:28). What does that mean for us today? It means that *hard work is foundational to being a successful woman.*

Hard work is a good and godly thing.

Since the Bible is clearly on board with women doing a variety of hard work, we should be too. You might be thinking, *Okay, what's the big deal? Our culture encourages women to do a variety of hard work too.* Great question. Yes, our culture encourages us, as women, to be ambitious in our plans and goals, but it doesn't take into account God's priorities for why we should work hard (we'll share that list with you soon!).

Contrary to modern culture, the purpose and motivation behind the labor of godly, hardworking women in the Bible was quite different. Almost without exception, these godly women worked hard for two reasons:

1. To glorify God.
2. To bless and serve their families.

Their purpose for working hard wasn't to exalt themselves. It wasn't to hang their achievements on a wall. It wasn't about becoming "something." It was rooted in glorifying God. It was centered in loving their families. It was consistent with God's design for femininity.

This Girl Has Ambition

The Proverbs 31 woman is the poster child when it comes to a selfless, hardworking woman. Although she wasn't a real woman, this chapter is a timeless picture of godly womanhood. In fact, Proverbs 31 was written as an example for Jewish boys to know what kind of qualities to look for in a wife. Proverbs 31:10–31 is written as a Hebrew acrostic for easy memorization. This example of an "excellent wife" not only shows men what a godly wife looks like, but it also gives women a clear picture of a God-defined woman.

The Proverbs 31 woman shows that ambition and hard work are high priorities for godly womanhood. Just reading about her makes the two of us dizzy. She was smart, industrious, business savvy, wise, loving, generous, talented, and diligent (just to name a few of her characteristics). She worked hard from sunrise to sunset and long into the night. She also worked inside and outside the home performing a variety of tasks. However, her work had very little to do with her.

As you read Proverbs 31, you'll quickly see why she worked so hard. Everything she did was for the same two purposes we just mentioned: to bring honor to God and to bless and serve her family. Her hard work (inside and outside the home) was centered around being a godly wife, mother, homemaker, and helper for her family. Her family and home were truly the center of her focus. Her work wasn't about her. It wasn't about her career. It wasn't about her independence. It was about honoring God and loving her family.

Serving our families, ministering to others, and glorifying God are foundational to becoming a successful woman.

The Proverbs 31 woman and other godly biblical women give us a good picture of what God-defined success looks like. *Serving our families, ministering to others, and glorifying God are foundational to becoming a successful woman.*

As the two of us began to understand God's heart behind hard work, a pressing question still lingered in our minds: *Should our specific design as females affect our life goals and plans? Should our womanhood cue us in on anything?* The culture was telling us it shouldn't, but we had a hunch God thought differently.

It's Time to Pull Out the Road Map

A long-standing joke between men and women is that men don't like to ask for directions and women do. Men have been known to drive many additional miles in order to avoid stopping for directions. Women, however, typically have no problem pulling over the car the moment they realize their course is unclear.

Although this is a humorous difference, it reveals an insightful contrast between the genders. Women love directions. We love to know where we're going and exactly how we're going to get there. We love having a plan.

When it comes to our womanhood, we (Kristen and Bethany) believe many of us have the same desire. We want a plan; we want directions. We want a road map for where we should be heading. We don't want to waste our time driving in circles.

Thankfully, God's got our back! He has given us, as women, the map to true and lasting success. In fact, our womanhood is such a big deal that he dedicates specific verses entirely to *us*.

Chapters like Proverbs 31 and Titus 2 give us a rock-solid standard of what it truly means to be successful.

Although every woman's life will look uniquely different, the principles found in these verses should be the foundation on which every woman builds her life. This is our road map. This is our guide.

We encourage you to read these directions carefully.

ROAD MAP TO GOD-DEFINED SUCCESS:

She fears the Lord (Prov. 31:30).

She speaks words of wisdom (Prov. 31:26).

She welcomes hospitality (Prov. 31:20).

She teaches with kindness (Prov. 31:26).

She takes great care of her home and family (Prov. 31:27, Titus 2:5).

She loves and respects her husband (Prov. 31:11–12).

She loves her children (Titus 2:4).

She's not lazy or idle with her time (Prov. 31:27)

She works really hard morning until night (Prov. 31:15,18).

She's respectful in her behavior (Titus 2:3).

She mentors younger women (Titus 2:4).

She's self-controlled in her words and actions (Titus 2:5).

She pursues purity in every area of her life (Titus 2:5).

God has a lot to say about womanhood. These verses make it clear that God-defined success isn't measured by how much money we make, how many degrees we've earned, how prestigious our career, how big we've grown our ministry, how many kids we've had, how large our house, or how fancy our car. God's standard for success is based on the condition of our hearts. He's looking for women who share his vision for womanhood, value the things he values, and pursue the things he loves.

If we want to be successful according to God's Word, we can't separate our femininity from our life plans. We can't separate our womanhood from our occupational goals. We can't plan our future and then try to squeeze biblical womanhood into it.

> *We can't plan our future and then try to squeeze biblical womanhood into it.*

For many Christian women, this is where the disconnect happens. Many of us know what the Bible says about womanhood, but we ignore it. We know what God's vision for success is, but we don't pursue it. Our head knowledge doesn't translate into life change. Without giving it a second thought, we place biblical womanhood in second place behind our ideas. This sad reality is most clearly seen when it comes to the topic of family.

Rethinking What You Value

Ladies, we can't beat around the bush. What the two of us are about to share isn't popular in our society. One of the most under-valued, under-pursued, and under-recognized career tracks today is becoming a wife and mother. Ask any college-age Christian girl today about her future plans, and rarely will she mention marriage and family. Why? Because those things aren't valued in our society anymore. They're not viewed as a successful plan. As a result, many young women are ashamed to verbally express their desire for them, much less plan for them.

This is a serious tragedy.

When we look at God's plan for marriage and motherhood, we see the complete opposite. God created marriage as a noble and glorious opportunity for men and women to showcase his character and nature. The gospel picture is intertwined throughout the marriage covenant of a husband and wife. In God's eyes, desiring to be a wife isn't a shameful thing but, rather, a highly honorable goal.

In addition to marriage, God loves children and motherhood. He places enormous value and respect on the home (Titus 2:4–5). As mentioned earlier in this book, God created us, as women, with a special ability to nurture relationships, produce life, and help others. Marriage, motherhood, and homemaking may be old-fashioned in some people's eyes, but they're honorable in God's eyes (Ps. 127:3–5; Prov. 18:22; 31:10–31).

> *In God's eyes, desiring to be a wife isn't a shameful thing but, rather, a highly honorable goal.*

Please know that we're *not* saying a woman's identity and value are based on her marital status or whether she is a mother. We are well aware that not every woman will get married and not every married woman will have children. We're simply making the point that God highly values these things; therefore, we should too.

I (Kristen) don't have kids yet, and Bethany isn't married, so it should be obvious that we believe God can use a woman in many ways. However, the two of us are passionate about valuing marriage and motherhood for one simple reason: because God does (Prov. 12:4; 17:6; 19:14).

As Christian women, we're called to be like him. If God values something, then we should too. If God calls something a blessing, then we should too. We should never be ashamed or embarrassed to love what God loves. Even if we never get married or have children, we should still champion these biblical truths.

Answering the Tough Questions

The topics of marriage, motherhood, and work inevitably stir up a lot of questions. We're guessing you have a few yourself. We've wrestled through a lot of tough questions, such as: "Is it wrong for women to strive for academic accomplishment?" "Is it wrong for Christian women to pursue a career?" "Is it wrong for moms to have a job outside the home?" These are great questions that demand solid answers.

In an attempt to get biblical answers to these pressing questions, we created a filtering system. We call it the "What, Why, and When Filter." By using this filter, we have been able to determine whether our specific plans and goals are biblical and honor God. This filter isn't foolproof, but it has helped us answer our tough questions, and we think it will help you too.

THE "WHAT, WHY, AND WHEN FILTER"

The What?

The first step to getting your answers is to start with the what. What do you want to pursue? What are you investing the majority of your time in right now? What are you striving to accomplish?

Is it a job? If so, what kind of job? Is it school? If so, what kind of degree? Is it marriage? Is it being a mom? Is it working in a ministry? Is it starting a business? What are you striving for?

Once you determine your what, the next questions to ask are these: Does my what allow me to serve and glorify God? Does my what violate any biblical commands or principles?

Whether it's a job, a degree, marriage, etc., your what should allow you to serve and glorify God and align with biblical commands. For example, if you get a job cashiering at a grocery store, there's probably nothing that would hinder you from serving and glorifying God. However, bartending in a raunchy club would definitely hinder you from serving and glorifying God. In that case, your what would need to change.

Here's the bottom line: If your what allows you to serve and glorify God, then you can move to the next step in this filter. If it does not, then you need to find a better what.

The Why?

The second step to getting your answers is to ask yourself *why*. You've already established your *what*, so now you need to figure out *why* you're doing it. Why do you want that job? Why do you want to go to school? Why do you want to get married? Getting to what's motivating you in your heart is key here. God is just as concerned about why you're doing something as he is about what you're doing.

We encourage you to genuinely search your heart and ask yourself why you want to do what you do. Is your motivation rooted in glorifying and honoring God? Is your desire to serve others?

When it comes to your why, the most important question is this: Is your motivation Christ-focused or self-focused?

Even good things can be pursued with a self-serving heart. For example, let's say you want to become a doctor. This is a good thing, in and of itself. But if your sole motivation for becoming a doctor is so people will praise you and give you accolades or so you will be make lots of money, then this is prideful, self-focused, and unbiblical motivation.

However, if your motivation for becoming a doctor is to serve others, share the love of Christ, and bring joy to your patients, then this is good and biblical motivation.

Here's the bottom line: if your why is Christ-focused and rooted in honoring God, then you can move to the next step of this filter. If it is not, then you need to reevaluate your why.

The When?

The third and final step to getting your answers is to ask yourself the when. You've already established your what and why, and now you need to determine whether the timing is right. This is where your when comes in.

Since life is made up of seasons, the timing of your choices needs to be carefully considered. The majority of people will go through the following three seasons:

1. A season of singleness.
2. A season of marriage.
3. A season of children living in the home.

Each season of life you're in should play a major role in your decision making. What you do and why you do it is just as important as when you do it.

For example:

Season 1: Singleness

The season of singleness is the most flexible season of the three. Without the responsibility of a family, a woman is able to invest much of her time in a variety of opportunities outside the home. If her what and why passed the test, then the next question should be, Is this the right when? In other words, Is this the best season to pursue _____?

Season 2: Marriage

This season brings on a new responsibility, which should reflect a new set of priorities. As we saw earlier in this chapter (as well as in chapters 5 and 6), God has given married women specific instructions for helping their husbands (Gen. 2:18) and taking care of their homes (Titus 2:5). This season is not quite as flexible as the season of singleness. As a married woman considers her what and why, she also needs to carefully take into account her when. Just because something is good, doesn't mean it's the best timing or season for it. Before taking on outside responsibility (assuming her husband is in support), a married woman needs to make sure she is first fulfilling her God-appointed role as helper and homemaker.

Season 3: Children Living in the Home

This season typically brings the greatest amount of domestic responsibility and is the least flexible of the three seasons. God places enormous value on motherhood, which is why he exhorts moms to love their children (Titus 2:4) and train them up in the way they should go (Prov. 22:6). Raising children biblically is a noble yet time-consuming calling.

Based on Scripture, we believe mothers with children living in the home should invest the bulk of their time and energy nurturing and raising them. Moms have been given a God-appointed role that is not intended to be passed off to others. With that being said, we recognize that some moms, due to uncontrollable circumstances, are not able to devote the amount of time they would like to homemaking and raising their children. However, each one of us, to the best of our abilities and resources, should strive to live out biblical motherhood.

And that is why this season is critical for considering your when. A good thing at the wrong time becomes the wrong thing. For example, if a mom with children living in the home is offered a job opportunity that will require her to spend nine to ten hours a day away from her children, then this job is probably not the best timing for her. The what and the why may be fine, but the when isn't ideal.

The two of us realize that this filter is not an easy process to work through–everybody's situation is unique. We also realize how countercultural much of what we're saying may be. But as we talked about earlier, God-defined womanhood is countercultural. It's radical.

Our hope is that this "What, Why, and When Filter" serves as a useful tool in helping you answer your difficult questions and navigate your future.

Planning Smart for Your Future

We often hear older women say they wish they could get a do-over regarding decisions they made when they were younger. As younger single women, they pursued their life goals without thoughtfully considering potential future seasons. Then ten years later, as married women, they found themselves trapped financially by overwhelming school loans, locked into their jobs, and unable to dedicate the time they would have liked to their husband and children.

In fact, a woman named Lindsey found herself in this very situation. As a college student, she didn't stop to consider what role marriage or motherhood might have in her future. She took out multiple school loans, pursued advanced degrees, and poured herself into her career. When she married her husband, Jeremy, she began to realize the value of a woman's role as helper and homemaker. Then, after she and Jeremy were married for two years, she got pregnant. Lindsey now desired to stay home and fulfill her God-defined role, but she couldn't because the couple had too much debt. She'll be the first to admit she wishes she had planned smarter.

So what's the lesson from Lindsey's story? Plan smart for your future. Looking back, Lindsey wishes she had pursued a less expensive route to earn her degrees (i.e., testing out of classes, learning through an online university, attending community college, etc.). She also wishes she and Jeremy had lived more frugally during their first two years of marriage and been more intentional about saving money.

Just like Lindsey, nobody knows what God has in store for the future. Therefore, it's wise to think about and plan smart for whatever roles God may call us to down the road.

Working with the Big Picture in Mind

Both of us pray your definition of a successful woman is being transformed. We hope you're catching a vision for how to measure your success according to God's design.

As Christians, we should never separate our earthly work from our spiritual work. We aren't just women, we're Christian women, and that means Christ goes with us everywhere. Our words, actions, ethics, and disciplines should reflect the image of Christ. Whether we're changing a diaper, leading a Bible study, or working in an office, everything we do should be for God's glory. The most successful women actively strive to merge their earthly work with their eternal value.

Life on this earth is short, and you only get one shot at it. What you choose to spend your time doing is one of the most important decisions you can make.

The most successful women actively strive to merge their earthly work with their eternal value.

We pray you'll set aside your desire to earn the praises of our culture and instead join the ranks of the hardworking women whose passionate desire is to glorify God. May all your work, from the smallest task to the largest, be a beautiful reflection of God-defined success.

CHAPTER 10

STUDY GUIDE

STASH IT IN YOUR HEART

The most successful women actively strive to merge their earthly work with their eternal value.

1. On the lines below, write down a one-sentence description of what you think a successful woman looks like.

   _____

   _____

2. Who or what has pressured you to become "someone"? How did you respond to that pressure?

   _____

   _____

   _____

3. The women we mentioned from the Bible (Ruth, Priscilla, and Lydia) worked hard for two reasons: (1) to glorify God and (2) to bless and serve their families. Below list how you work hard for each of these reasons.

   1. To glorify God.

   _____

   _____

2. To bless and serve your family.

_____

_____

4. How should your design as a female affect your life plan?
   Write down one verse to support your answer.

_____

_____

_____

5. Are you hospitable to God's design for the wife and mother?
   If not, your heart does not align with God's. What changes
   do you need to make in order to value those roles (now or
   in the future)?

_____

_____

_____

MAKE IT HAPPEN *Today*

Open your Bible and read Proverbs 31:10–31. Pick one quality you
can put into practice today.

Part 4

CHOOSING TO BECOME
A GIRL DEFINED BY GOD

11. BRAVE ENOUGH TO CHANGE YOUR LOOK

I (Bethany) scanned the addresses as Kristen slowly drove through the unfamiliar neighborhood. We were looking for a two-story house with a redbrick front and a minivan in the driveway.

"Oh, there it is! And . . . there it goes. We just missed it," I said to Kristen as we passed by our destination.

We backed up, and Kristen pulled into the driveway. We were meeting a group of women to carpool across Texas to a conference. As we got out of our car, I started regretting my decision. *Why would I agree to travel across the state to a women's conference with a bunch of ladies I don't even know?* I thought to myself. I was starting to feel uncomfortable, and I began to wish I'd stayed home. I wasn't familiar with the conference speakers, and I'm honestly not sure how the two of us ended up going (outside of God's providence, of course).

The drive to the conference was much less awkward than I had anticipated. The ladies who carpooled with us were talkative, sweet, and extremely relaxed. We arrived at our hotel, quickly freshened up, and then rushed to the conference center to find seats. "Wow! There are a ton of women here. I had no idea it was going to be this big," I whispered to Kristen as we took our seats.

The next few days left us feeling like someone had dropped a bomb on us. A really good bomb. The kind of bomb that explodes your thinking and challenges you to make radical changes in your life. For the first time in our lives, we heard women share their thoughts on topics like feminism and the truths of God-defined womanhood. Neither of us had ever attended a conference with such bold, unapologetic teaching on biblical womanhood.

Overwhelmed is the best word to describe how we felt at the end of that conference. The things we learned were similar to what we'd already read, studied, and discovered about biblical womanhood—only on steroids. It was teaching powerful enough to transform a woman's life. There was no light and fluffy talk inside those conference walls. The speakers shared hard-to-swallow truths with no hesitation.

When we left the conference, we both faced the same dilemma. Do we take these powerful rock-our-world truths and put them into action, or do we leave this new knowledge in our heads? That simple decision would make all the difference in our lives. Everything we learned at the conference would do us zero good if we didn't do the hard work of putting the truth into practice.

And that's exactly where this chapter finds you. Understanding God-defined femininity and actually living it out are two totally different things. Biblical knowledge without application is useless.

Biblical knowledge without application is useless.

Trust us, we get it. Applying the truths of biblical womanhood is not easy. It's countercultural. Unpopular. Challenging. Uncomfortable. And just plain out of our natural sinful inclination. And that is why most Christian women never transfer the head knowledge to the heart. It's just too hard. It takes too much work and doesn't receive praise from others.

Say No to the Wimpy Woman

Put all your other thoughts aside and pretend the two of us are having a personal conversation with you. We understand this struggle. We get how hard it is to put truth into action. We've been there many times and still face that fight today.

It's easy to get pumped about measuring success according to God's Word, until you walk out the front door and come face-to-face with women who demean God's view of success. It seems thrilling to apply true love to your romantic relationships, until the guy you're dating disagrees and you are left single or fighting for true love on your own. It feels somewhat easy to reject the pillars of counterfeit femininity, until you feel the rush of the cultural current pushing you in the wrong direction. It's easy to focus on God's bull's-eye for biblical womanhood, until you look around and realize you are the only one aiming your arrows in that direction.

Author and teacher Mary Kassian uses the term *wimpy woman*, which has been a huge eye-opener for us. What is a wimpy woman? We're glad you asked. A wimpy woman gives up on biblical femininity when life gets hard. A wimpy woman quits when she has to stand alone. A wimpy woman caves in when the culture pressures her. A wimpy woman rejects her distinct role as a female when her husband (or boyfriend, brother, father, etc.) doesn't fulfill his role. A wimpy woman doesn't put her head knowledge into action because it's just too hard.

A wimpy woman gives up on biblical femininity when life gets hard.

The Choice Is Yours

When the two of us left that women's conference, we had a choice to make. We could wimp out by continuing to live as if we'd learned nothing new, or we could bravely face these radical truths and apply them to our lives. It wasn't easy, but God gave us the strength to continue to conform our lives according to his design.

It takes a strong woman to acknowledge God's Word and an even stronger woman to actually live out what he teaches. Brave women only. The question is this: Will you be a brave woman? Will you trust God at his Word and faithfully obey what he teaches about femininity? Will you follow after him even if no one else does?

A brave woman does exactly what Kim Wagner describes in her book *Fierce Women*. A brave woman "grabs the hem of God's will and doesn't let go."[1] That's what it takes to be a brave woman. It takes guts, gumption, and a whole lot of trust in God. It takes a willingness to look dumb in the world's eyes in order to look wise in God's eyes. It takes a brave woman to wholeheartedly chase after God's design.

Brave

God is looking for women who will be *brave* in today's society. We're challenging *you* to be one of those women. To be one of the few who are willing to liberate yourself from the commonality of wimpy womanhood. Our generation is in need of Christian women who are willing to rise up and show the culture the powerful influence a God-defined woman can have.

We're going to take you through an easy-to-understand acrostic of the word *brave*. Here's what a brave woman looks like:

B = BOLD

Boldness. This is something I (Kristen) was missing when I was seated at that table I described in chapter 10. I was afraid of what that female doctor would think of me. I didn't want to mention anything that would make her have a low opinion of me. I was wimpy and too focused on her opinion instead of God's.

A bold woman doesn't shy away from questions pertaining to her femininity. A bold woman confidently lives out her design as a nurturer, helper, and life producer with no apologies. A bold woman is unafraid of what others may think of her.

I (Bethany) understand God's high view of marriage and motherhood and desire to embrace those roles some day. Sadly, though, because our culture places little value on those roles, I used to feel embarrassed and ashamed to admit my admiration for them. Instead of boldly sharing my true feelings and finding confidence in God's Word, I would often wimp out and try to please those around me.

When it comes to your design as a woman, don't wimp out. Don't be afraid of what others may think of you. Embrace God's truths and confidently share them when the time is right. Be a bold woman who stands up to the bully of counterfeit femininity. Be bold in defending the value of marriage and motherhood. Be bold in defending modesty and the dignity of a woman's body. Be bold in declaring your faith in Jesus Christ.

R = RADICAL

The word *radical* is often associated with something extreme or different. That's a great description of what we, as Christian women, are called to be. The moment a woman trusts Christ as her personal Savior is the moment she takes on a radically different purpose. Her life is no longer about pleasing herself; it's about living to please God. That, in and of itself, is radical.

Being radical isn't a new concept—we see it throughout the Bible. Romans 12:2 makes it very clear that Christians should be different. "Do not be conformed to this world, but be transformed by the renewal of your mind, that by testing you may discern what is the will of God, what is good and acceptable and perfect."

The two of us have learned to be okay with living radically different lives than those around us. The older we've gotten, the easier it has become. We've learned to accept the fact that we are different. We are different in the way we talk, dress, interact with men, engage in media, view the home, live out gender distinctions, and on and on. We are radical, and we are okay with it.

Are you okay with being radical? Are you okay with looking extreme or different in the eyes of those around you?

The next time you are faced with a decision to either follow the culture's path or obey God's Word, remember the word *radical*. Remember that Jesus was radical during his thirty-three years on earth. He can sympathize with you. He can relate. If you are scared of being radical, talk to him. He can understand you better than any human and give you the strength to live a radically different life.

A = ANCHORED

The word *anchored* is a perfect description of our friend Lynn Marie. Lynn Marie is a woman anchored in God's Word. She studies it, memorizes it, and believes it. Her mind is so filled with truth that she can spot a lie a mile away. She isn't easily swayed by the pressures of our culture because she's anchored in truth. Lynn Marie is a living example of Psalm 1:1–3:

> Blessed is the man who walks not in the counsel of the wicked, nor stands in the way of sinners, nor sits in the seat of scoffers; but his delight is in the law of the LORD, and on his law he meditates day and night. He is like a tree planted by streams of water that yields its fruit in season, and its leaf does not wither.

Even though the psalmist used the word *man* and male pronouns, these verses apply to all Christians. This passage is a perfect description of what it looks like to be anchored in

God's Word. We are called to be like a strong tree planted by the river.

If you meditate on God's truth daily, you will not be easily swayed. When the storms of life hit you, you will be able to withstand the pressure. Being anchored in God's Word will give you the power to boldly and radically live out your femininity. If you truly believe God's Word is the final authority, then make a habit of studying it. Understanding God's truth and being anchored in his Word can give you true power to live out God-defined womanhood.

V = VIGILANT

I (Kristen) am not a passionate hunter, but as a girl born and raised in Texas, I've done it once or twice. One scorching-hot Texas day, Zack took me hunting. During the hunt I had to be completely focused. I had to be totally silent and ready. I had to be 100 percent alert at all times.

That is exactly how we, as Christian women, must live. Alert, watchful, and ready! The moment we let our guard down is the moment the enemy, Satan, will strike. The Bible says, "Be sober-minded; be watchful. Your adversary the devil prowls around like a roaring lion, seeking someone to devour" (1 Pet. 5:8).

The idea of you living out God-defined femininity drives Satan crazy. He hates God and wants you to do a poor job of reflecting him. The battle is real. You must be on guard. You must be vigilant against the enemy's attacks.

In our experience, Satan's attacks have been sneaky and subtle. They've come through the media and through the pressure from those around us.

We encourage you to focus on God's Word and keep a careful watch for the enemy. Your design as a woman is worth fighting for.

E = EMPOWERED

When I (Bethany) was in seventh grade, I did something that shocked an entire gymnasium full of people, including myself. My siblings and I were at an open gym, playing pickup games with the neighborhood crew. Besides my sisters and my mom, I was the only girl in the gym.

I was minding my own business, shooting around a basketball, when an obnoxious younger guy came over and started demanding that I give him the ball. I looked at this squirt and said, "No, I'm using this ball."

With a shocked look on his face, he replied loudly, "That's my ball! I brought it, and I want it now."

I knew the ball belonged to the gym, so I told him no. I guess he wasn't used to being told no, so he went off on me. He started yelling and stomping his feet. He even threw a chair on the ground. He was causing a huge scene, and the entire gym paused to watch.

Instead of giving in to this guy's tantrum, I threw the ball down the court in the opposite direction of him, smiled, and then walked away. The onlookers erupted in applause. I later figured out that this guy was a bit of a troublemaker, and the regulars were proud I didn't give in to his obnoxious intimidation. I can only laugh at myself now. The skinny little blonde girl standing up to the basketball dude. What a sight!

In a funny sort of way, that is exactly how we, as Christian women, need to be. We need to know the truth about and have confidence in our womanhood. When the world stomps its feet and rages against our decision to live out biblical womanhood, we can feel empowered to stand strong. God's Word is the final authority and contains all the power we need. The more you study the truth and understand God's design, the more empowered you will be. When your friends question you, you will be prepared to defend what you believe. The truth is empowering. With it you will have the strength to stand up to anyone.

Will You Be a BRAVE Woman?

Are you ready to join the ranks of brave women in our generation? Are you ready to put truth into action and show the world how to do womanhood right?

We came up with a fun test to help you find out just how brave you really are. Grab a pen and paper or use your phone to record some numbers. You're going to rate yourself in regard to each letter from the word *brave* on a scale of 1–10, with 1 being the lowest and 10 the highest. At the very end you will add up your score. Ready? Let's see how you measure up.

BRAVE TEST

B = BOLD
On a scale of 1–10, how bold are you in living for the approval of God and not those around you?

1 ... 2 ... 3 ... 4 ... 5 ... 6 ... 7 ... 8 ... 9 ... 10

1-4 Not bold. I am very concerned about what people think of me.
5-7 Sometimes bold. I want to live for the approval of God, but I still care about pleasing those around me.
8-10 Very bold. Living for the approval of God is my highest priority.

R = RADICAL
On a scale of 1–10, how willing are you to look extreme or different in the eyes of those around you?

1 ... 2 ... 3 ... 4 ... 5 ... 6 ... 7 ... 8 ... 9 ... 10

1-4 Rarely ever. I want to blend in. I don't like standing out.
5-7 Occasionally. If the circumstance is obviously wrong.

8-10 Almost always. I'm willing to follow Christ regardless of how extreme I may look.

A = ANCHORED

On a scale of 1–10, how anchored are you in God's Word and understanding his truth for femininity?

1 ... 2 ... 3 ... 4 ... 5 ... 6 ... 7 ... 8 ... 9 ... 10

1-4 Not anchored. I don't read my Bible often. I don't understand God's design for femininity.
5-7 Here and there. I read my Bible at least once a week and have a basic grasp of biblical femininity.
8-10 Firmly grounded. I strive to read my Bible daily and actively live out biblical womanhood.

V = VIGILANT

On a scale of 1–10, how vigilant are you in looking for deception and lies, pertaining specifically to God's design for your womanhood?

1 ... 2 ... 3 ... 4 ... 5 ... 6 ... 7 ... 8 ... 9 ... 10

1-4 Very distracted. I don't give a lot of thought to worldly influences in my life.
5-7 Somewhat aware. I catch the obvious lies but don't proactively look out for them.
8-10 Highly on guard. I keep a careful watch for deception and lies.

E = EMPOWERED

On a scale of 1–10, how empowered and confident do you feel in standing up for God-defined femininity?

1 ... 2 ... 3 ... 4 ... 5 ... 6 ... 7 ... 8 ... 9 ... 10

1-4 Weak and uncertain. I am not strong when it comes to standing up for God-defined femininity.

5-7 Fairly confident. I'll stand up for the truth as long as it's not too much of a risk.

8-10 Extremely confident. Because of God's Word, I feel empowered to stand up for God-defined femininity.

Alrighty girl! Once you add up your scores, take your total number and compare it to the correlating paragraph below to see how you did.

1-10 You are really struggling. You could use a major overhaul in your life. You need to get into God's Word and study, study, study. Take some time to figure out the truth about your femininity and grow in your understanding of the Bible.

10-20 You need more confidence. You have some good head knowledge, but you are too scared to live it out. The culture's pressures intimidate you, and you are too wimpy to fight. You wish you could embrace God's design, but you don't make studying the Word your priority. Pick a letter from the word *brave* and start working on it today.

20-30 Things are so-so. You desire to live out godly femininity, but the culture's influence is too prevalent in your life. Get rid of unbiblical messages and start replacing them with truth. Evaluate your media habits and friend choices and make sure you are surrounding yourself with people and things that push you toward truth.

30-40 Way to go, girl. You are doing better than most out there. You have a desire to apply and live out truth, and we are proud of you. We can't encourage you enough to continue growing in your knowledge of God's Word and studying biblical womanhood. Buy another book on biblical womanhood (*Let Me Be a Woman* by Elisabeth Elliot is a great one!), find a mentor, start a Bible study—keep learning. You are doing great!

40-50 You are doing awesome! You have a strong desire to serve God, no matter the cost. You aren't concerned about looking popular in the eyes of others. You are focused on living for God's glory. We challenge you to take this message of God-defined femininity and spread it far and wide. Don't keep it inside. Use the wisdom God has given you to challenge other women.

Raising the Bar

Brave women are needed like never before. Will you rise to the challenge? It's time to show the culture what a real woman looks like. With God's help, *we can do it!*

CHAPTER 11
STUDY GUIDE

It takes a strong woman to acknowledge God's Word and an even stronger woman to actually live out what he teaches.

1. You have learned a lot over the past eleven chapters. Check off two words that best describe how you are feeling:

   ☐ Overwhelmed

   ☐ Excited

   ☐ Discouraged

   ☐ Refreshed

   ☐ Intimidated

   ☐ Hopeless

   ☐ Guilty

   ☐ Energized

   Why are you feeling that way?

   _____

   _____

   _____

2. In what areas of your life do you tend to be a wimpy woman? Circle all the areas that need strengthening.

179

I tend to be a wimpy woman . . .

    In my romantic relationship (marriage or boyfriend)

    At my job

    In my media choices

    On my phone apps

    In choosing good friends

    In my weekend habits

    At church

    At the parties I choose to attend

    In how I deal with my kids

    When it comes to how much I read my Bible

    In moments when I know I should say no

    Other_____

Look at which ones you circled. Why are you being a wimpy woman in those areas? What needs to change for you to be a brave woman?

_____

_____

_____

3. How can you be a brave woman and put what you've learned into action?

_____

_____

_____

4. How did you do on the brave test? Write down one way you can put each of the five words into action.

B = BOLD _____

R = RADICAL _____

A = ANCHORED _____

V = VIGILANT _____

E = EMPOWERED _____

MAKE IT HAPPEN *Today*

Grab a note card and on it write down the acrostic *brave* with each correlating word. Place the card somewhere you will see it on a regular basis.

12. TURNING HEADS
IN A NEW DIRECTION

"Ow, ow! Look at you go, girl!" I (Kristen) said to Bethany as she strutted past me in her high heels.

"This feels so weird," Bethany said, laughing as she tried to keep her balance. "I've never worn heels this tall before! I feel like a skyscraper." We both laughed.

I finished strapping the buckles on my high heels and then jumped up to join her on her catwalk. "This feels awesome!" I said while strolling past her.

This scene is a flashback moment of the two of us in high school. As tall girls, we rarely wore high heels. Um, scratch that. We *never* wore high heels. So one day we decided to buy some really tall ones just for fun. After practicing how to walk, we took our skills out on the town.

"Let's go to the mall and walk around!" I said enthusiastically.

"Perfect," Bethany responded, applying extra makeup. We hopped in the car and made a beeline for our destination.

After securing a parking spot, we proudly strutted into the mall. With our heads held a little higher than usual, we unashamedly made our way through various stores. We weren't shopping to buy stuff, we were shopping for attention. We smirked at each other as many glances and stares came our way. We felt like models on a runway and secretly hoped everyone else thought we looked like models too. Our vanity meter was about to explode. We soaked up the attention and relished every moment. In our minds, the spotlight was on us, and we were basking in it.

Living for the Glances

We can't help but roll our eyes when we think about that day at the mall. Thankfully, by God's grace, we've matured a lot since then.

Although we don't strut around the mall in high heels anymore, our vanity and pride haven't disappeared. As we've matured, our strategies for seeking glory and attention have simply been refined. We're going to be totally honest with you. The two of us battle against our prideful, selfish hearts every single day. We always struggle with wanting to turn heads in our direction. We're constantly fighting to give God the glory. We fight hard to keep Jesus at the center of our thoughts.

Here's proof. Just recently, I (Bethany) rushed through my busy day doing a lot of "good" stuff. I spent time with my little sisters, helped my dad with his business, and even worked on writing this book. I looked like an awesome Christian to everyone who saw me! But when my head hit the pillow that night, I suddenly realized a sad reality. I rushed through my entire day without devoting a single second to praying, reading my Bible, or even mentioning God's name. I was a good Christian girl doing good things. That's it. I honestly wasn't doing it for God though. I was doing it for myself. I was proudly parading through my busy day, giving little thought to my Creator.

The two of us have a hunch we're not alone in this struggle. The tendency to live life independently of God is a constant battle because of the human heart, which is sinful. Can you relate? Sadly, as Christian women, we often don't take the time to slow down and recognize this problem. We spend weeks, months, and even years pouring our lives into a bottomless jar. We live for temporary moments, giving little to no thought of eternity.

I was proudly parading through my busy day, giving little thought to my Creator.

The harsh reality is that when we don't live our lives for God's glory and purposes, we live in vain. Imagine how wasteful our lives would be if we spent every day sashaying around the mall in heels. That seems obvious, right? Well, when we're living for something other than Christ, we're basically doing the same thing.

Up until this point in the book, you've read about some amazing truths regarding your womanhood. However, promoting biblical womanhood is not the primary reason we wrote this book. We wrote it because we're passionate about God's glory. And because we're passionate about God's glory, we're passionate about the things he values. And because we're passionate about the things he values, we're passionate about biblical womanhood. Make sense?

As you read this chapter, know that the two of us are in the trenches with you. Living for God's glory isn't a piece of cake for us. We're writing these truths from our hearts, which are consistently being refined by God.

You're Actually a Model

The moment you became a Christian, your entire life took on a whole new meaning. You instantly joined a new family. You became an adopted child to a new Father. You gained new siblings. You received new family rules. You acquired new desires. You became an heir of a new future. Your adoption changed everything.

185

As a result of this monumental moment, you received a brand-new identity. You're no longer just a woman—you're a *Christian* woman. Your life is no longer defined by the culture—it's defined by God. That fact should radically change every aspect of your life. Instead of living to put yourself on display, you are now called to display the character and nature of your Creator.

Ephesians 5:1–2 says, "Therefore be imitators of God, as beloved children. And walk in love, as Christ loved us and gave himself up for us, a fragrant offering and sacrifice to God."

Did you catch that? You're called to *imitate* God as beloved children. The word *imitate* actually means "to mimic or model." Do you realize what that means for you? The moment you became a Christian you also became a *model*! If you've ever dreamed of becoming a model, your dream has become a reality. You are a model of God.

So what is the primary job and responsibility of a model? Think about it. If a fashion designer hires a model, what are they hoping to accomplish? Well, they want the model to make their clothing look good, right? And if she does a good job displaying the clothing, it will reflect well on the clothing's designer.

If you do an excellent job modeling Christ, you will honor God and positively reflect his image.

Are you seeing the parallel here? You have the same job. As a Christian, you're called to model your life after the life of Christ. Your goal should be to model the same actions, love, and character Christ displayed when he walked this earth. If you do an excellent job modeling Christ, you will honor God and positively reflect his image. If you do a poor job, you will reflect an inaccurate and unappealing image of your Designer to those around you. Being a model isn't a piece of cake though. There's a lot at stake.

Okay, so what's the big deal? you might be wondering. *What's the worst that can happen if I don't do a good job modeling Christ in the world?* We have wrestled with these same questions. The second half of Ephesians 5:2 offers some insight about why it's such a big deal. It says, "And walk in love, as Christ loved us and gave himself up for us." Did you catch that last part? "Gave himself up for *us.*" Let's make that a little more personal. Insert your name on the blank line: "Gave himself up for _____."

Jesus Christ, the King of the universe, came down to this earth to suffer and die for *our* sins. He loved us so much that he was willing to die for us. And he died for us so we can spend eternity with him in heaven.

And that is why we must be passionate about accurately modeling Christ. The gospel message is at stake by the way we, as Christians, live. If we're not actively displaying Christ, the gospel will not be reflected through our lives.

> *If we don't model Jesus to the lost world around us, who will?*

Here's the kicker: If we don't model Jesus to the lost world around us, who will? When we take a step back and look at the bigger picture, it's easy to see how the gospel is at stake if we don't live for God's glory.

We Are His Representatives

"This is really awkward," I (Bethany) said as I pulled a vacuum cleaner out of the backseat of the car. "I can't believe I'm doing this!"

"They don't have a clue," Kristen responded while glancing toward the house.

Kristen and I unloaded our cleaning supplies and then slowly made our way to the front door.

Ding dooooong. After thirty seconds, a nice old grandpa opened the door.

"Oh, come on in!" he said excitedly. "Hey, Johnny, the cleaning ladies are here!" he yelled to his little grandson.

Kristen glanced at me, and then we both gave him a friendly smile. This was us venturing outside our comfort zone. Way outside.

At this point in time, we were both in our early twenties and working in our family's business. When our parents first moved to San Antonio back in the 1980s, they started a business cleaning houses as a way to make ends meet. Well, the business took off and has been growing ever since. Kristen and I have worked on and off in the office answering phones, doing web work, and training employees. However, this particular day was different. We were thrown a major curve ball.

Somehow the schedule got overbooked, and several customers were left without house cleaners. We tried to reschedule their appointments, but nothing worked out. There was only one option left: *Kristen and me.*

We were terrified because we had *never* gone into someone's home to professionally clean it. We knew how to train the employees . . . but getting out there and doing it ourselves was a different ball game. We packed a set of cleaning supplies, each put on a green "White Glove Maid Service" T-shirt, and headed to the customer's house.

And that brings us back to the beginning of this story.

Kristen and I unloaded our supplies in the house, talked to the customer for a few minutes, then quickly got to work. We spent the next three hours working as a team to thoroughly clean the two-story house. Let's just say we looked a lot more professional than we felt.

Kristen and I knew we had to do an over-the-top job. We knew the quality of our work was a direct reflection on the family business. How the customer felt about us was how he would feel about the entire company. We were the physical representatives for the whole operation.

Thankfully, we did a good job. We think. He didn't complain at the end, so that's a good sign. That day marked the beginning and end of our professional cleaning careers.

We are sharing this story because it's the perfect illustration for how real life works. As Christian women, we are acting as representatives as well. Our lives are a direct reflection of the One for whom we work and serve.

When Christ ascended back into heaven after his resurrection, people could no longer observe his life to see how he lived. He was no longer physically present to show the world

As Christian women, we are acting as representatives as well.

his truth. He had a plan though. He put his children in charge of representing him. That includes you, girl! We are now in charge of representing Christ to the world. We are responsible for reflecting an accurate picture of the "family business," so to speak. We are in charge of reading God's Word and living out his truths.

Second Corinthians 5:20–21 says, "Therefore, we are ambassadors for Christ, God making his appeal through us. We implore you on behalf of Christ, be reconciled to God. For our sake he made him to be sin who knew no sin, so that in him we might become the righteousness of God."

The word *ambassador* is key here. It means "an authorized messenger or representative." When you became a Christian, you joined a new family to become a messenger and representative of Christ himself. You are now responsible for representing him to your family, friends, co-workers, church, and everyone else who sees you. God has commissioned you to bring the gospel message with you everywhere you go (Mark 16:15).

God has commissioned you to bring the gospel message with you everywhere you go.

In fact, God actually placed you in your sphere of influence for that very reason. The family you grew up in wasn't an accident. The siblings you have aren't a mistake. The husband and children you serve are opportunities to showcase Christ's love. Regardless of how easy or difficult your family circumstances may be, you can bring the power and hope of the gospel into those spheres.

For Such a Time as This

Let's look at the story of Esther in the Old Testament for an example of how one woman quickly learned the importance of her sphere of influence. Esther was a Jewish orphan living under the care of her cousin Mordecai in the land of Persia (Esther 2:7). The king of the land wanted a new queen, so he gathered beautiful young virgins into his royal harem. Esther was chosen and taken away (v. 8). She was probably scared to death the day those soldiers snatched her out of normal life and took her to the king's palace to be a concubine.

As her future unfolded, she soon found herself queen of Persia (v. 17). The king chose Esther to be his new queen above all the other virgins. Little did she know that with her new title, she would be forced to make some extremely tough choices. Choices that would threaten her very existence.

The king's highest and most powerful official, Haman, was plotting to kill all the Jews throughout the land (Esther 3:6). Although Esther's Jewish identity was still a secret, she knew Haman's plot would mean certain death for her people . . . and possibly for herself.

As she wrestled with the life-threatening circumstances before her, she probably wondered why God had put her in that position (Esther 4:11).

Mordecai reminded her of God's bigger plan: "For if you keep silent at this time, relief and deliverance will rise for the Jews from another place, but you and your father's house will perish. And who knows whether you have not come to the kingdom for such a time as this?" (v. 14).

Esther responded to Mordecai's counsel by asking all the Jews to fast alongside her for three days. At the end of the three days, she made the courageous choice to place her life on the line in hopes of saving God's people (vv. 15–17).

Esther was placed on this earth and commissioned by God for "such a time as this."

Just like Esther, God has placed you on this earth during this time period, in your country, in your city for *such a time as this*. God handpicked you to come into this world exactly when you arrived. You aren't here by accident. You are here on a God-defined assignment. You're right where you are on purpose and for a purpose.

We (Kristen and Bethany) don't know the ins and outs of your personal life, but God does. Maybe that hard-to-love parent was put in your life for *such a time as this*. Maybe that difficult sibling was put in your life so you could show them Christ's love. Maybe that hard-to-please boss was put in your life so you could share the gospel with them. Maybe you experienced those unexpected single years so you could serve God in a more focused way. Your circumstances might be tough, but if you step back and look at the bigger picture, you just might be in them for *such a time as this*.

You are here on a God-defined assignment.

Are you willing to serve God right where you are? Right now? Are you willing to bring the gospel into your sphere of influence? Are you willing to reflect the nature of Christ through your God-defined femininity? Are you willing to model biblical womanhood to a lost and confused society?

191

Living for the Forever

Once during a road trip, the two of us went into a Caribou Coffee coffeehouse and both noticed the company's tagline. It reads, "Life is short. Stay awake for it." Of course, this tagline is referring to coffee and caffeine, but it unintentionally points to a deeper truth.

Not many people like to think about the end of their lives. Not many people like to think about dying. But the truth is life is short. Very short. We don't have time not to think about it. As Christian women, we can't make the drastic mistake of sleeping through life. We have to live our lives wide awake and focused on God's bigger plans and purposes for us. We have to live our lives with forever in mind.

Once our lives on this earth have ended, there's no turning back. We can no longer make changes. There are no redos. One life. That's all we get. And how we live that one life on earth will have an impact on how we spend all of eternity.

When we die, we will each stand before the judgment seat of God. Not to be judged for our salvation (Christ already died for us) but for how we lived on this earth. We will stand individually before our Creator and give an account of our entire lives. "For we will all stand before the judgment seat of God. So then each one of us will give an account of himself to God" (Rom. 14:10, 12 NASB).

Then God will reward us for the lives we lived for him. "For we must all appear before the judgment seat of Christ, so that each of us may receive what is due us for the things done while in the body, whether good or bad" (2 Cor. 5:10 NIV). You will receive what is "due" to you based on how you lived. Your obedience to God on this earth will impact how you spend all of eternity.

If you take a step back and look at the bigger (eternal) picture, you will quickly realize why your womanhood is so important. You only get one shot at doing things right. You only get one life to live for Christ. Every minute, hour, day, and year that passes can never be reclaimed. Your choices matter. That is why we are so passionate about the message of God-defined womanhood.

As we have shared throughout this book, we've seen far too many Christian women fail to serve Christ. We've seen far too many Christian women fall prey to counterfeit femininity. We've seen far too many Christian women pour their entire lives into a bottomless jar. We don't want this to happen to you. We don't want it to happen to us. Since no one can know when their last day on this earth will be, we must be intentional with the time we have. Our days are already numbered by God.

The fact that you're reading this book right now proves God isn't done with you. He has work for you to do on this earth. You are alive right now because he has a God-defined assignment for you to fulfill. He wants to use you in a powerful way to display his glory and gospel to everyone who sees you. He wants to use your life to model the character and nature of Christ in your sphere of influence and turn heads in a new direction.

You are God's earthly representative. You are alive for such a time as this. The question is this: Will you obey him? Will you choose to live your life for his glory and not your own? Will you choose his design for your womanhood over the influences of secular culture? Will you be brave?

When forever comes, only the things you did for Christ will truly matter. Everything else will fade into the background. As C. T. Studd so wisely writes in his poem "Only One Life, 'Twill Soon Be Past," "Only what's done for Christ will last. And when I am dying, how happy I'll be, if the lamp of my life has been burned out for Thee."

When forever comes, only the things you did for Christ will truly matter.

Our prayer is that each one of us will catch and nurture an eternal vision for life. May we not waste one day. May we not waste one opportunity. Make it count. When forever comes and our short lives on this earth are done, it will have been well worth the effort.

CHAPTER 12
STUDY GUIDE

When forever comes, only the things you did for Christ will truly matter.

1. Can you think of a specific time when you intentionally tried to turn heads in your direction? If so, what did you do?

   _____

   _____

   _____

2. Does the fact that you're a model of Christ impact the way you want to live? What changes do you need to make to reflect a more accurate picture of Christ?

   _____

   _____

   _____

3. You have been placed in your sphere of influence for "such a time as this." What difficult circumstances (or people) are you facing today? How might you bring the love of Christ into that situation?

   _____

   _____

   _____

4. If you were to interact with someone who didn't already know you were a Christian, would your words, actions, and attitudes be an obvious reflection of Christ? Why or why not?

_____

_____

_____

5. Imagine yourself standing before the judgment seat of God. How do you think you will be rewarded based on how you lived your life on earth? What changes should you make today to avoid regrets later?

_____

_____

_____

MAKE IT HAPPEN *Today*

Write down three ideas about how you can start living for forever. Put one of those ideas into action today.

_____

_____

_____

Part 5

FEMININITY WORTH FIGHTING FOR

13. IMAGINE THE POSSIBILITIES

I (Bethany) scanned the shelves in Mrs. Meyers's living room and noticed they were filled with trophies.

"What are these for?" I asked, pointing to the shelves.

Mrs. Meyers looked in my direction and said, "Deary, these are my dancing trophies. I was a swing dancing champion for ten years in a row. You should have seen the way I moved. Oh, I used to tear up that dance floor." She gazed off into the distance and looked as if she were daydreaming.

I quickly got the impression her trophies were her most prized possessions. It seemed as if she was holding on to the memories and clinging to the happy feelings she recalled from that time in her life.

"I remember spending holiday after holiday competing in the national competition. My poor children had to spend the majority of those holidays alone with their dad. I guess that's the price one pays for being a champion. In the end, as you can see, I won the trophies, but I'm starting to wonder if it was worth it." Mrs. Meyers's smile slowly faded as she finished talking.

After a few more minutes of chitchat, I got down to business. I was at her house for my dad's senior care company. Mrs. Meyers was in her late eighties and needed regular assistance. My job was to get the papers signed and help her feel as comfortable as possible. The meeting flew by, and before I knew it I was waving good-bye through my car window.

Several months after that initial meeting, I heard my dad on the phone talking with one of the senior care employees. He asked if she was available to work Christmas Eve and Christmas Day. Apparently, Mrs. Meyers's children were too busy to make the trip down to visit her. I can't help but wonder if her absence during their childhood was the reason for their absence in her old age.

It appeared that Mrs. Meyers had spent the majority of her holidays alone in her old age. No turkey dinners surrounded by family. No sharing favorite holiday memories over freshly baked pie. No traditions. Nothing to look forward to or prepare for. Just watching the same old holiday specials on TV.

Can you picture that? Can you imagine spending your holidays alone?

Kristen and I are deeply saddened by Mrs. Meyers's story. She spent the best years of her life investing in temporary things that did not last. "But lay up for yourselves treasures in heaven, where neither moth nor rust destroys" (Matt. 6:20). We can learn from her story and start planning now for a less lonely and empty future.

Imagine what could happen if you lived with your eternal home in mind.

Our prayer is that all women will invest their lives in something bigger than collecting trophies. The two of us want you to imagine the possibilities for what your legacy could hold. Imagine a different ending than the one Mrs. Meyers and many others are leaving behind. Imagine what could happen if you lived with your eternal home in mind.

Now we want to introduce you to three women who have lived their lives for a greater purpose. They each have very different stories and very different legacies. These women are unique in their own way, but each one is creating a future and a legacy that will last beyond their earthly home.

Say Hello to Mrs. Harris

Chloe's skin-tight leather pants, paired with her bright pink hair, made quite the introduction. Chloe was a bad girl desperately trying to turn good. She was a lost and broken mess in search of help. Without immediate intervention, the downward spiral Chloe was following in life would have spun completely out of control. And that's where the hero, Mrs. Harris, comes into play.

Let's switch scenes and get a little background on our key player.

Mrs. Harris was happily married at a young age. Before she had children, she and her husband turned their home into a shelter for lost and broken girls. Girls who were drug-addicts, pregnant, or runaways. What was Mrs. Harris's goal? To mentor, love, and disciple these young women. She wanted to show these hurting girls God's love in a real and tangible way.

Mrs. Harris continued her open-home ministry until she became pregnant and had a baby of her own. At that point, she and her husband decided to close their doors to estranged girls. They both agreed that investing their time in the lives of their own children would be their primary ministry. Over the next thirty years, Mrs. Harris poured her life into training up and discipling her children. She viewed them as future husbands, wives, fathers, mothers, leaders, and influencers, and she wanted to make sure they were given the best foundation possible to build on.

Mrs. Harris wasn't focused on the here and now. She had a generational vision and wanted to leave behind a legacy that wouldn't fade with time. She wanted her legacy to reflect her investment in people rather than things.

Mrs. Harris is now an empty nester and a widow. According to the world's standards, she should be moving into a season of full-time rest and relaxation. She's paid her dues and is now entitled to a life of "me time" with long walks on the beach and gardening. As lovely as that may sound, it never crossed her mind.

Mrs. Harris knows she is alive and kicking for a greater purpose. She doesn't want to waste any part of her life or miss a single opportunity to serve God. She recently decided to reopen her home to struggling girls. And that's where pink-haired Chloe comes back on the scene.

Chloe was lost, confused, and seriously in need of counseling. She walked into a church hoping someone would be willing to help her. That's when she met Mrs. Harris, who invited Chloe to live with her. Over the next year and a half, Mrs. Harris devoted her life to mentoring, discipling, and loving Chloe. The change in Chloe's life wasn't instantaneous, but it was happening. Slowly but surely she let down her guard and fell on her knees and cried out to God. Her life was being transformed right in front of Mrs. Harris's eyes.

> *She had a generational vision and wanted to leave behind a legacy that wouldn't fade with time.*

Neither Mrs. Harris nor Chloe would have guessed what was about to happen. Jake, Mrs. Harris's nephew, was beginning to grow deeply attracted to Chloe. Jake saw the change in Chloe's heart as she grew in her relationship with Christ. He thought her spiritual transformation was beautiful. Long story short, Jake fell in love with Chloe and asked her to be his wife. Last we heard, they had five beautiful children and were both faithfully serving God.

Mrs. Harris is a picture of a woman who is using her life to the fullest. Because of this one woman's faithfulness and long-term vision, many generations have been and will continue to be influenced for Christ.

All of this was possible because one woman was willing to serve God.

Just think of the many girls she has mentored over the years. Each one was changed for the better because of her willingness to nurture relationships and produce spiritual life.

All of this was possible because one woman was willing to serve God. One woman was willing to live with eternity in mind. One woman was willing to be brave and live out biblical womanhood.

Why We Love Mrs. Harris's Story

Mrs. Harris was just a regular wife and mother, yet she left an incredible legacy. So often we, as Christian women, look at the great heroes of the faith and feel like we need to do something big to make an impact. Not true. Mrs. Harris wasn't a famous missionary. She wasn't a popular speaker or well-known author. She was just an everyday woman married to an everyday man with an everyday family. And because of her willingness to live for God's purposes, he used her to make an extraordinary impact in the lives of countless others. Mrs. Harris will leave behind a legacy that reaches far beyond anything she ever could have imagined.

That is the kind of legacy the two of us want to leave, and we hope you do as well.

Let's pause and take a quick trip into the future. Imagine yourself twenty years down the road. What do you see? Do you see yourself as a Mrs. Harris or more of a Mrs. Meyers? Do you see yourself creating a legacy that will reach into eternity?

Our prayer is that all Christian women will have the mind-set of Mrs. Harris. To be women who invest in the people around them. Women who serve their families. Women who live under the reality that this is not their forever home. We, as faithful followers, are simply ambassadors for Christ, passing through on our way to heaven. If we can embrace that mind-set, we will no doubt leave behind a legacy that will last for generations to come.

Anna's Shattered Heart Restored

The yelling escalated, followed by a plate crashing against the wall. Anna put her hands over her ears, trying to block out the horrific sound. She hated that her dad treated her mom and siblings this way. She also hated when she was the target of his explosions. This was her life though. It was all she knew.

Anna grew up in a supposedly Christian family. They went to church on a weekly basis, the children attended a private Christian school, and everyone appeared to have it all together. Sadly, it was all a facade. Behind closed doors, their home was anything but loving. Anna's dad put on the face of a Christian in public but took it off at home. His abusive words and actions left the family terrified.

As Anna entered her early twenties, she was totally turned off by the idea of marriage and starting a family of her own. She wanted nothing to do with a husband. She had experienced a living nightmare growing up and couldn't understand why God designed men to be the leader in marriage. She assumed all men used their strength to harm others, and she never wanted to be in that position again. Marriage and motherhood were definite nos in her mind.

Anna quickly settled into her adult life as an independent single woman. She researched a church to attend and was able to get involved right away. Within the first few months of attending her new church, Anna saw godly men and women doing marriage God's way. She saw men protecting and serving their families. She saw wives helping their husbands and investing in those around them.

Eventually, God softened Anna's heart and opened her eyes to the beauty of doing things according to his design. She finally realized that her dad was not following God's design for manhood and, as a result, was hurting those around him.

Anna realized she needed to make radical changes in her heart attitude if she truly wanted God's best for her life. She didn't want her past to distort her view of truth or her hope for the future.

She assumed all men used their strength to harm others, and she never wanted to be in that position again.

One late summer night, Anna fell to her knees and surrendered her life to God. She prayed and asked him to help her value what he values. She asked him to soften her heart toward his truth. She confessed her lack of belief in his design of manhood and womanhood and asked him to give her a desire for God-defined femininity.

Sometimes answers to prayer come quicker than expected. Before Anna had time to process everything God was doing in her life, Mr. Right came knocking on her door.

After many conversations and lots of prayer, Mr. Right asked Anna to be his wife. She and her husband, Jared, were married on a picture-perfect spring day.

The Power of a Reclaimed Life

Despite Anna's difficult upbringing, she has been able to overcome her fears and trust God for her future. The Bible has become her standard for truth and the source of all wisdom.

Even though Anna is young, her legacy is already forming. Her decisions are positively impacting her husband, three children, friends, and family. Her younger siblings are constantly challenged by the way she has chosen to forgive their dad. Anna's life brings mountains of hope to any woman who has experienced pain and suffering. Her life is a model for what can happen when a woman fully surrenders herself to God.

It's amazing how one woman's choices can affect current and future generations. Imagine where Anna would be if she had chosen to reject God's design and hold on to bitterness. She certainly wouldn't be where she is today. Thankfully, she chose the opposite route and is creating a legacy that will not fade with time.

> *It's amazing how one woman's choices can affect current and future generations.*

Sadly, the two of us know many Christian women who are in less-than-ideal situations. Whether it's physical or verbal abuse, an absent parent or husband, or divorce, we can't deny that Christian women are facing hardships. If you are in—or have come from—a painful situation, we want you to know we are burdened for you. We are so sorry you have had to endure pain because of the sinful choices of others.

Our prayer is that you will read Anna's story and find hope for your future. We want you to know it is possible—by God's grace—for you to have a purposeful and God-honoring legacy. If you are willing to choose forgiveness and trust that God's design truly is best, you can also reclaim the life God has given you.

To help guide you through this, we've written a prayer in the next chapter that will help you surrender your life to God (see page 221).

Sarah's Choice to Leave It with God

Sarah was sick of guys, and she was sick of the way she fell head over heels every time she received attention from them. Her life was structured around how to grab the next guy's eye. And it was wearing her down to the bone. After another major breakup and pillow-sobbing session, Sarah hit rock bottom. Would this always be her life? Living from guy to guy? Surely God had a better plan.

In a moment of brokenness and desperation, she dusted off a book she had nearby and flipped to a page. The quote at the top of the page read, "God always gives his best to those who leave the choice with him."[1]

Tears fell from her eyes as she realized how far she had fallen from that truth. She wasn't leaving the choice with God. She was doing her best to control her life, guarding the reins firmly in her own hands. That day marked a turning point. That night she made a commitment before God to give him the reins and live for his purposes, not her own. No more chasing boys. No more living for the moment. No more wasting the precious hours and days God was giving her. She wanted God's best for her life and knew she would have to completely surrender to him for that to happen.

She wanted God's best for her life and knew she would have to completely surrender to him for that to happen.

Sarah is now twenty-nine years old. Her life has taken some drastic turns over the past ten years and is nothing like she imagined it would be when she was younger. God had a very different (but very good) plan in mind for Sarah. Because of her willingness to trust God with her future, he has used her in surprising ways. One of the most exciting prospects came when she least expected it. These opportunities were nowhere on her radar, but they were definitely on God's. He had been preparing her for "such a time as this."

It was a hot summer day when she got the call.

"Hello, my name is Jane Sanders, and I heard about you through a mutual friend. I know you don't know who I am, but I have something I'd really like to discuss with you."

Sarah was intrigued and said, "Yes, I'd love to hear about it."

Jane continued on.

"I've worked in a well-known publishing company for several years. I'm always on the hunt for new authors and book ideas. I'm intrigued by your life as a single girl, and I would love to discuss the details of putting your story into book form. Is that something you'd be interested in?"

Sarah was stunned and shocked and absolutely interested. She had always enjoyed writing but had never considered publishing a book. She took some time to pray and was quickly convinced this was an opportunity straight from the hand of God.

Only days after verbally agreeing to write the book, she received the official contract in the mail.

Sarah's book is now published and in stores all across the world. As a result of her book, God has brought dozens of opportunities for her to travel and speak to groups of young women. Sarah's faithfulness as a single woman has inspired many Christian girls to give their futures to God and use their single years to serve him.

Sarah had no idea her simple decision to leave the choice with God would bring her such purpose and fulfillment. She had no idea God's work would be this evident in her life.

To this day, Sarah doesn't know if she will ever get married. She also isn't sure if she will publish more books. Her future plans are uncertain, but her goal is set in stone. She desires to live to the fullest by influencing those around her. She is determined to leave an eternal legacy in whatever way God sees fit for her to do so. She is willing to do whatever God asks of her for "such a time as this."

This is a shout-out to all the single girls. Take comfort and hope in Sarah's story. You don't have to be married to create a lasting legacy. Sarah is almost thirty years old, single, and creating a legacy that will endure. God will use your life as well if you are willing to do what Sarah did—leave the choice with God. He will bring opportunities you never even knew existed.

You don't have to be married to create a lasting legacy.

We challenge you to write down this quote and make it true for you: "God always gives his best to those who leave the choice with him."

Join Sarah and make that your heart's cry. Leave the choice with God, and watch as your legacy begins to form.

Your Legacy Begins Now

The three women you just read about have inspired the two of us to take action and live as ambassadors for Christ. We hope they have done the same for you.

It's time to start setting up your future for success by making the necessary changes today. Don't wait to reach the next season of life to start creating your legacy. If God can use a widow, a young mom, and a single girl, imagine how he could use you.

CHAPTER 13
STUDY GUIDE

Your future legacy is being created today through the people you serve, the choices you make, and the way you invest your time.

1. Is the way you're living now going to produce results more like those of Mrs. Meyers or Mrs. Harris? Why?

   _____

   _____

   _____

2. What is on your to-do list each day? Quickly jot down the top ten things that consume the majority of your time each week.

   1. _____

   2. _____

   3. _____

   4. _____

   5. _____

   6. _____

   7. _____

   8. _____

9. _____

10. _____

Now scan your list and circle only the things that will leave behind a lasting legacy.

3. Like Anna, are there people in your life whom you need to forgive? Are you allowing those people's sins to hinder you from creating a God-honoring legacy?

_____

_____

_____

4. Who are the women in your life you can look up to as examples of how to leave a legacy? What about their lives inspires you?

_____

_____

_____

5. "God always gives his best to those who leave the choice with him."

Like Sarah, is there something in your life you need to leave in God's hands? What is it? What prevents you from surrendering that area to God?

_____

_____

_____

_____

_____

MAKE IT HAPPEN *Today*

Write down two or three sentences describing the legacy you want to leave behind (e.g., "I want to be a woman remembered for . . .").

_____

_____

_____

14. LET'S GET THE SISTERHOOD STARTED!

Our dad stood at the front of the family room with a serious look on his face. He had called a meeting earlier in the day, and the two of us along with our five other siblings gathered nervously. Whenever our dad called a meeting, we assumed it was to discuss something wrong we had done.

"I called this meeting to talk about something very important. I've been thinking about this for quite some time, and I've decided to bring it to your attention."

With a smile creeping up the corners of his lips, he said, "Coming this summer, you will each gain [insert long dramatic pause] a brand-new sibling!" He and our mom grinned as they watched our excited and surprised faces.

"Yeah! This is awesome. I can't wait!" I (Bethany) excitedly cheered at the news.

"I can't believe you kept it a secret for this long. Are we going to find out if it's a boy or a girl?" Kristen asked.

Our parents answered with a resounding no! The entire family would have to wait until the baby was born to find out if we would gain more "girl power" or more "boy power."

At this point in time, we (Bethany and Kristen) were in early high school, and the girls were winning by one. The boys were eagerly rooting for a boy to even the scales. If the guys' wish came true, then we would finally be on an even playing field. Four boys and four girls. If it was a girl, our home would become an estrogen powerhouse.

If it was a girl, our home would become an estrogen powerhouse.

When the long-awaited day finally arrived, we all gathered nervously in the living room and waited and waited and waited. Babies just never seem to be in a hurry.

Oh, and did we mention that our mom was a baby-birthing pro? She birthed the rest of her babies at home beginning with me (Bethany). And this baby was no exception.

After what seemed like an eternity of waiting, we soon heard a baby's cry. The cry was quickly followed by a loud shout from our dad: "It's a girl!" Those were the words we had been waiting for. The boys (Michael, Stephen, and Timothy) gave each other looks that said, "Oh dear. We are going to be overrun by estrogen." The girls (Ellissa, Rebekah, and the two of us) exchanged happy glances that said, "Oh yeah, baby. Girls rule the house now."

When the scales tipped in the girl direction, our new sister, Suzanna, made sure they tipped hard. She has proven over the years to be the most girly girl of us all. She loves pink, sparkles, and all things tulle. She has unashamedly lived up to her title "girl."

Growing up in a family of five girls—plus our mom and all our female pets—has been quite the ride. The two of us love each one of our sisters and have created a bond that will last forever. We are sisters by birth, and we are also sisters in Christ. There is no experience quite like it.

The benefits of being in a sisterhood are priceless. The emotional support (which we need a lot of) and spiritual encouragement have made us incredibly close.

Sisters are like best friends whom you can never get rid of. They are there to laugh with you, cry with you, and sometimes laugh *at* you. They are God-given teammates, and we wouldn't trade them for the world.

Let's Get the Sisterhood Started

Can we get an "amen" from all the sisters out there? We're talking directly to you, girl. Yep, sisters in Christ all the way. We may not be related by birth, but we are related through the blood of Christ. We, as Christian women, are going to spend eternity together with our Father in heaven. We can honestly say we will be sisters forever.

Let's be real for a minute. Living out what the two of us have written in this book is not easy. We need the support and strength of one another. And that's exactly what the sisterhood is for. The sisterhood is the Christian woman's secret weapon for success. If we band together and fight for one another, we will grow God's kingdom and be strengthened to live out biblical womanhood for the long term.

When the mighty forces come against God-defined femininity, our sisterhood will remain like a rope with many cords.

When the mighty forces come against God-defined femininity, our sisterhood will remain like a rope with many cords. We won't be weakened. We won't be broken. We will be stretched and pulled but not destroyed.

God describes the benefits of the sisterhood perfectly. Here's what he has to say (although this verse uses male pronouns, the truths still apply to us):

Two are better than one, because they have a good reward for their toil. For if they fall, one will lift up his fellow. But woe to him who is alone when he falls and has not another to lift him up! Again, if two lie together, they keep warm, but how can one keep warm alone? And though a man might prevail against one who is alone, two will withstand him—a threefold cord is not quickly broken.

Ecclesiastes 4:9–12

That is the mantra of the sisterhood. If one falls, the other will be there to pick her up. If one is cold, the other will be there to keep her warm. If one is attacked, the other will be there to help her fight.

"Woe to him who is alone when he falls." Don't be that loner. Don't try to live out your womanhood on your own. Join the sisterhood and find strength in its numbers.

Sadly, many women want you on their team but are not committed to doing things God's way. You will be pushed and pulled in the wrong directions. You won't be challenged spiritually, and you won't be strengthened. Instead, you will be weakened by their sisterhood.

We want you to know that the true sisterhood of Christian women will not pull you down. The sisterhood that the two of us are part of isn't built on man-made ideas. This sisterhood is built on the foundations of God's Word and made up of women who are desperately dependent on God for courage and strength.

The true sisterhood is banding together for biblical womanhood. We (Kristen and Bethany) are here to be your sisters. We are here to encourage you—to pick you up spiritually and give you the courage to fight for truth.

The Power of One Woman

"You're not going to believe this!" I (Kristen) said to Bethany as we sat at my breakfast table.

"What is it?" she asked, glancing up from her laptop computer.

"We just got an email from a publishing company, and they're interested in publishing a book with us!" I replied, wide-eyed.

"What?" she asked as her mouth dropped open.

That is the beginning of how this book ended up in your hands today. The two of us had launched GirlDefined Ministries only eight months before that email came in.

Our personal journey with our ministry has opened our eyes to some amazing truths about God. The biggest lesson we've learned is that God doesn't need an army to accomplish his work; he just needs a few faithful followers.

When we launched the ministry, we had very little money, very little experience, and very little website knowledge. We trusted God and left the results to him. And boy did he surprise us.

Less than one year after launching, unimaginable doors of opportunity opened. God multiplied our meager efforts. Our "five fish and two loaves" turned into dozens. Within a year of launching, we landed the publishing deal for this book, flew several times around the country for speaking opportunities, published our content for large Christian outlets, received hundreds of emails from girls around the world, and had our blog posts translated into more than a dozen languages.

> God doesn't need an army to accomplish his work; he just needs a few faithful followers.

Our eyes were opened wider than ever before to God's awesomeness. He isn't looking for the smartest, the prettiest, the coolest or the richest—he is looking for the willing. He is looking for the faithful. He is looking for small groups of people who are ready to serve him (John 14:12). We (Kristen and Bethany) aren't sharing these things with you to brag. We're sharing them with you to show you how amazing God is. If he is willing to use two average girls from Texas, he is willing to use *you*. God specializes in the minority.

217

The Bible is exploding with examples of how God used the nobodies to accomplish big things. Think of Esther. God used her to save thousands of Jews (Esther 8:1–17). Think of Rahab, the bad girl gone good. God used her in the lineage of Christ (Matt. 1:5). Think of Mary. God used a teenage girl to bring the Savior of the world to this earth (Luke 1:30–33). These were average everyday women. They were girls just like you. Just like us. God didn't use them because of how extraordinary they were. He used them because of how obedient their hearts were.

When one woman is willing to obey God, the results can be earth-shattering. Generations can be changed forever. Lives can be impacted for all of eternity.

> When one woman is willing to obey God, the results can be earth-shattering.

In a culture in which most women are rebelling against God's design, God is looking for those who will be faithful. He is looking for those who will go against the grain and obey his Word. Second Chronicles 16:9 says, "For the eyes of the LORD run to and fro throughout the whole earth, to give strong support to those whose heart is blameless toward him."

God sees you. He sees us. He is watching the entire earth for any woman who is willing to serve him. Doing great things for God starts today. It starts right here—in our small sisterhood. God will use you in a mighty way if you're willing to be obedient.

Will You Join the Sisterhood?

Have you ever jumped off a cliff? The two of us have. Okay, it was more like a small cliff. Well, it was more like a teeny tiny cliff. But still . . . we took the leap to land in the refreshing water below.

There's always that moment of truth, right? That scary ten seconds as you stand on the edge and peer into the water. You know what we're talking about. Everyone starts pressuring you from behind, yelling, "Jump, jump!" Your knees start shaking as you realize there's no turning back. In order to avoid wimp status, you have to jump. You hold your breath and take a leap of faith. Then, *splash*! You hit the water. Everyone cheers from the top. You did it! And it was worth it.

As you finish reading this book, it's like you're standing on top of the cliff. You've hiked a long way to get here, and now you're at the top. You're looking down into the water and wondering if you should take the leap. The two of us are behind you cheering, "Jump, jump!" We want you to take that leap of faith and join us in the sisterhood.

Following God's plan for womanhood may seem scary at first. In fact, taking that first jump is always the hardest. It requires the most faith. You're not doing this alone though. God will help you every step of the way. We will cheer you on through our prayers.

If you're ready to take that jump and join the sisterhood of God-defined femininity, we have a challenge for you. Read the following "Girl Defined Challenge" and check off all the boxes of the things to which you're committed.

GIRL DEFINED CHALLENGE

I am committed to becoming . . .

☐ A strong woman who allows God's Word to define my purpose in life.

☐ A woman who boldly lives out God's design for my gender role.

☐ A woman who is committed to displaying biblical femininity through my words, actions, and clothing choices.

☐ A woman who makes it a priority to help others, produce life, and nurture relationships.

219

☐ A woman whose value and worth is found not in my outward appearance but in my relationship with God.

☐ A woman who is known for showing genuine *agape* love in my romantic relationships.

☐ A woman who works hard at everything I do for the purpose of serving others and glorifying God.

☐ A woman who is BRAVE.

☐ A woman who lives life with eternity at the front of my mind.

☐ A woman who will leave behind a godly legacy for many generations to come.

God asked the prophet Isaiah, "Whom shall I send, and who will go for us?" Isaiah responded by saying, "Here I am! Send me" (Isa. 6:8). Our prayer is that you would be a woman in the twenty-first century who says the same thing. "Here I am! Send me." God desires to do powerful things through your life for his glory. God desires to multiply your meager fish and loaves and turn them into something extraordinary.

The two of us pray you will join the sisterhood as we humbly say to God, "Here we are! Send us."

Finishing Strong

Every good fairy tale starts with four little words: "Once upon a time . . ." When we, as females, hear those words, we get excited. We love a good fairy tale. Starting a story well is important, but it's not nearly as important as how the story ends. A strong ending makes the entire story complete.

Right now, you are in the middle of your story. You can look back on your life and see the beginning. You can see what your story looks like today. The only thing you can't see is how it's going to end. Although you don't know exactly how your story will end, you've already been told what the best ending looks like. You've already been given the final key words.

Just as fairy tales always start with four key words, your life story should end with six key words. Do you know what they are? These final six words should be the goal of every Christian's life. *"Well done, good and faithful servant"* (Matt. 25:23). As a Christian woman, your entire life should be lived with the purpose of hearing those final six words.

Your story is being written right now. The choices you make today will affect how it ends. Early in this book we explained the tragic life story of Marilyn Monroe. Her choices as an adult did not enable her life to end well. If you desire a better outcome for your story as a woman, you must choose a better path. If you want your story to have a strong ending, you must choose to live according to God's design. Honor him with your life. Reflect him through your womanhood. Cherish him with your words. Praise him through your actions. Surrender your will to his.

We (Kristen and Bethany) are so grateful you've taken this journey with us! As we come to a close, we want to leave you with a powerful prayer of surrender. This is the constant prayer of our lives. We encourage you to write this prayer down and pray it regularly.

Dear heavenly Father,

Thank you for your amazing design of my womanhood. Thank you for handcrafting me in my mother's womb and bringing me into this world right when you did. I know I am here on a God-defined assignment. I submit my life, my goals, and my plans to your design. I surrender my will to yours. Please give me the courage to be a brave woman in these modern days. Give me strength to reflect your character in every area of my life. I love you and am humbled to be called your daughter. May I live my life to one day hear you say, "Well done, good and faithful servant." Amen.

May you never lose sight of what really matters in this life. May you never underestimate the power one woman can have. May you never grow weary of reflecting Christ through your womanhood.

Our world desperately needs to see Christian women who have a backbone and are willing to say no to evil and yes to righteousness. Will you be à God-defined woman?

CHAPTER 14

STUDY GUIDE

STASH IT IN YOUR HEART

Our world desperately needs to see Christian women who have a backbone and are willing to say no to evil and yes to righteousness.

1. Are there women in your city who can act as your local sister-hood? If so, how can you encourage, challenge, and pray for one another on a regular basis?

_____

_____

_____

2. In this chapter you read Ecclesiastes 4:9–12. In your own words, describe the importance of not living the Christian life alone.

_____

_____

_____

3. How has this book had an impact on your view of woman-hood? What is the most powerful thing you've learned?

_____

_____

_____

4. Are you living your life with the purpose of hearing, "Well done, good and faithful servant"? Why do you think it's important to one day hear those final words?

_____

_____

_____

5. If you have benefited from the wisdom in this book, don't keep it to yourself! Can you think of one friend who would benefit from the message of biblical womanhood? If so, we challenge you to do one of the following:

   • Buy her this book and explain how it has inspired you.

   • Invite her to read it alongside you and discuss the book together.

MAKE IT HAPPEN *Today*

Are you committed to actively living out the ten points from the Girl Defined Challenge? If so, we invite you to join the sisterhood by signing your name below.

ACKNOWLEDGMENTS

We (Kristen and Bethany) love reading books. As young teenagers, we devoured every Christian book we could get our hands on. As we hit our early twenties, the idea to write a book of our own slowly crept into our minds. We began jotting down some notes and tossing around ideas. God knew we weren't ready though. Instead of opening doors of opportunity right away, he took us through five long years of writing boot camp. We filled our computers with tens of thousands of words. Then we erased those words and started over again. Then we erased those words and started over *again*. We wrote and rewrote our book ideas until God knew we were ready. When the timing was right, he opened doors of opportunity that we never could have imagined. With the support, prayers, encouragement, and chocolate chip cookies from our family and friends, the two of us ventured to write this book. The journey was hard (like pull-your-hair-out hard), but God helped us cross the finish line! And we are so grateful. Please join us in applauding those who helped make this book become a reality.

God . . . thank you for giving us the Bible—our ultimate guide to life, our greatest resource, and the foundation for the pages in this book. Thank you for giving us your Son—our Savior—the reason we have hope, purpose, and joy on this earth.

Dad and Mom . . . our lifelong supporters and the reason this book exists. Without your love, support, wisdom, and constant encouragement, we would have given up years ago. Thanks for always believing in us.

Zack . . . our all around go-to guy. Your ability to fill so many different roles has blessed our socks off! From late-night book edits to latte runs, you've been an adviser, technology expert, and so much more. We are grateful for all of your help and support.

Stephen, Ellissa, Timothy, Rebekah, and Suzanna . . . y'all are the bomb. Thanks for loving us, encouraging us, and taking over all of our jobs and family duties during this project. The freshly baked cookies, home-cooked meals, and coffee runs kept us alive.

Michael and Jamie . . . your constant prayers and delicious lunch provisions were so important. And, baby Hadley, your sweet kisses were irreplaceable.

Clark Family . . . thanks for being there for us at the very beginning of this project as we scrambled to write chapter 1 on our trip to Colorado. Your constant encouragement, prayers, and high fives kept us going during the lonely days of "Girl Defined prison."

Girl Defined Prayer Team . . . your prayers were answered, and this book is the proof. We treasure each one of you.

Nicci Jordan Hubert . . . you are incredible. Thank you for pouring your time and energy into this book. You made this process fun and practically painless.

Rebekah Guzman . . . your initial contact with us was an answer to years of prayer. Thanks for helping us accomplish a lifelong goal. We can't say thank you enough.

Baker Books . . . thank you for believing in us and giving us this opportunity.

Erin Davis . . . thank you for answering dozens of questions and pointing us in the right direction.

Friends who supported us along the way . . . you kept us sane. We love you!

NOTES

Chapter 1 Bullied by the Big Bad Checklist

1. Elisabeth Elliot, *Let Me Be a Woman* (Carol Stream, IL: Tyndale, 1976), 52.
2. Susan Hunt, *By Design: God's Distinct Calling for Women* (Franklin, TN: Legacy, 1994), 17.

Chapter 2 Blonde Bombshells Don't Have What It Takes

1. C. S. Lewis, *Mere Christianity* (New York: HarperCollins, 1980), 50.

Chapter 3 Counterfeit Femininity, You've Done Me Wrong

1. *Merriam-Webster OnLine*, s.v. "liberation," accessed October 6, 2015, http://www.merriam-webster.com/dictionary/liberation.
2. Margot Peppers, "'Models Are Some of the Most Insecure People I've Ever Met': Miranda Kerr on How She Has to Practice Loving Herself," *Daily Mail*, October 1, 2013, http://www.dailymail.co.uk/femail/article-2440134/Miranda-Kerr-Models-insecure-people-Ive-met.html.
3. Betsey Stevenson and Justin Wolfers, *The Paradox of Declining Female Happiness* (Cambridge, MA: National Bureau of Economic Research, May 2009), http://www.nber.org/papers/w14969.pdf.
4. Anna Pasternak: "Fast Track to Femininity: Why Competing with Men Has Left Women Out of Touch with Their Feminine Side," *Daily Mail*, June 2009, http://www.dailymail.co.uk/femail/article-1039030/Fast-track-femininity-Why-competing-men-left-women-touch-feminine-side.html#ixzz3Pb9DDfr2.
5. C. S. Lewis, *The Weight of Glory* (New York: HarperCollins, 1980).

Chapter 5 Gender, You Are Oh So Magnificent

1. Jenny Soffel, "Swedish Preschool Takes Aim at Gender," *The Star*, June 23, 2011, http://www.thestar.com/news/world/2011/06/23/swedish_preschool_takes_aim_at_gender_stereotypes.html.

2. Mary A. Kassian and Nancy Leigh DeMoss, *True Woman 101: Divine Design* (Chicago: Moody, 2012), 27.

Chapter 6 Modern Chic, Meet Biblical Womanhood

1. Got Questions, How Was the Woman a Helper Suitable for the Man (Genesis 2:18)?, accessed November 12, 2015, http://www.gotquestions.org/woman-helper-suitable.html#ixzz3U7Z6ccvI.

2. *Merriam-Webster OnLine*, s.v. "helper," accessed October 9, 2015, http://www.merriam-webster.com/dictionary/helper.

3. Kassian and DeMoss, *True Woman 101*, 85.

4. Elliot, *Let Me Be a Woman*, 61.

5. Kassian and DeMoss, *True Woman 101*, 189–90.

6. Ibid., 74.

7. Eun Kyung Kim, "Chatty Cathy, Listen Up: New Study Reveals Why Women Talk More than Men," *Today*, February 21, 2013, http://www.today.com/health/chatty-cathy-listen-new-study-reveals-why-women-talk-more-1C8469360.

Chapter 8 Beauty That Doesn't Need a Runway

1. "I Gave Up Modeling for God," *New York Post*, April 24, 2013, http://nypost.com/2013/04/24/i-gave-up-modeling-for-god/.

2. "Am I Beautiful," YouTube video, 46:40, from an Am I Beautiful Event at the Hangar of First Baptist Church Spartanburg on May 16, 2013, posted by "fb spartanburg," May 22, 2013, https://www.youtube.com/watch?v=2-lGIpiBpwQ.

3. Elyse Fitzpatrick, *Idols of the Heart* (Phillipsburg, NJ: P&R, 2001), 23.

Chapter 9 When True Love and Femininity Collide

1. "16 Signs It's Time to Move On and End the Relationship," Love Panky, accessed October 13, 2015, http://www.lovepanky.com/love-couch/broken-heart/16-signs-its-time-to-move-on-and-end-the-relationship.

2. "No One Said Finding the One Would Be Easy," *Daily Mail*, January 1, 2014, http://www.dailymail.co.uk/femail/article-2532213/No-one-said-finding-The-One-easy-The-average-women-kiss-FIFTEEN-men-enjoy-TWO-long-term-relationships-heart-broken-TWICE.html#ixzz3UrcWnulD.

3. Christopher Ingraham, "Divorce Is Actually on the Rise, and It's the Baby Boomers' Fault," *Wonkblog* (blog), *Washington Post*, March 27, 2014, http://www.washingtonpost.com/blogs/wonkblog/wp/2014/03/27/divorce-is-actually-on-the-rise-and-its-the-baby-boomers-fault/.

4. For more information on Ian and Larissa Murphy, please see their website Ianandlarissa.com/.

5. Paul E. Eymann, "What Is True Love and How Do You Know When You've Found It?," Christian Answers Network (Gilbert, AZ: Christian Answers Network, 1996), http://www.christiananswers.net/q-dml/dml-y030.html.

6. John Piper, *What's the Difference? Manhood and Womanhood Defined according to the Bible* (Wheaton, IL: Crossway Books, 1990), 23.

7. Mary A. Kassian, *Girls Gone Wise in a World Gone Wild* (Chicago: Moody, 2010), 120–21.

8. Sheila Gregoire, "People Are Watching Your Marriage," *To Love Honor and Vacuum* (blog), accessed October 12, 3015, http://tolovehonorandvacuum.com/2011/10/on-affection-dealing-with-teenagers-and-successes/.

Chapter 10 Hardworking Women Doin' It Right

1. "The World's Most Inspiring Women," *Forbes*, July 17, 2010, http://www.forbes.com/2010/07/17/role-model-oprah-winfrey-angelina-michelle-obama-forbes-woman-power-women-jk-rowling.html.

2. Nancy Leigh DeMoss, ed., *Becoming God's True Woman* (Wheaton, IL: Crossway, 2008), 16.

Chapter 11 Brave Enough to Change Your Look

1. Kim Wagner, *Fierce Women: The Power of a Soft Warrior* (Chicago: Moody, 2012), 21.

Chapter 13 Imagine the Possibilities

1. Jim Elliot, *The Journals of Jim Elliot*, ed. Elisabeth Elliot (Grand Rapids: Revell, 1978).

KRISTEN CLARK is married to her high school sweetheart, Zack, and is the cofounder of GirlDefined Ministries. She is passionate about promoting the message of biblical womanhood through blogging, speaking around the country, mentoring young women, and hosting Bible studies in her living room. In the end, she's just a fun-lovin' Texas girl who adores all things outdoors and eats dark chocolate whenever possible.

BETHANY BAIRD is a Texas girl doing life with her parents and seven siblings. She is the cofounder of GirlDefined Ministries and is passionate about spreading the truth of biblical womanhood through blogging, speaking, and mentoring young women. To her family and close friends, she is simply a tall blonde girl who loves any form of competition, drinks way too much coffee, and can't get enough of her little fluffy dog.

Continue learning about God's design for women . . .

Visit GirlDefined.com for blogs, resources, and more from GirlDefined Ministries.

 contact@girldefined.com

 @Girl_Defined

 GirlDefined

 GirlDefined

@ GirlDefined

LIKE THIS
BOOK?
Consider sharing it with others!

- Share or mention the book on your social media platforms. Use the hashtag **#GirlDefined**.

- Write a book review on your blog or on a retailer site.

- Pick up a copy for friends, family, or strangers! Anyone who you think would enjoy and be challenged by its message.

- Share this message on Twitter or Facebook: **"I loved #Girl-Defined by Bethany Baird and Kristen Clark // GirlDefined.com @ReadBakerBooks "**

- Recommend this book for your church, workplace, book club, or class.

- Follow Baker Books on social media and tell us what you like.

 Facebook.com/ReadBakerBooks

 @ReadBakerBooks